The
New Chic

The New Chic

French Style from Today's Leading Interior Designers

Marie Kalt and the editors of *Architectural Digest* France

RIZZOLI NEW YORK

New York Paris London Milan

Contents

The New French Chic

France and interior design have a long history together. Just in the twentieth century, we find a long succession of designers who, decade after decade, defined the French sense of taste and made it a worldwide standard. From Émile-Jacques Ruhlmann to Armand-Albert Rateau, Jean-Michel Frank to André Arbus, Madeleine Castaing to Henri Samuel—not to mention Jacques Grange, François-Joseph Graf, and Jacques Garcia, the internationally renowned heirs of French *haute décoration*—the list continues to grow. All of these designers, in their own way, have left their stylistic mark on an era, inspiring subsequent generations.

When I arrived at *AD* magazine in 2008, we took up the question of who would become the next prominent figures in this long and illustrious history. After the early 2000s, when the press focused primarily on furniture and object design, a discipline in which French designers also play a leading role around the globe, we felt the importance of reviving interest in the French tradition of interior design, and of identifying the emerging talents who would become the stars of tomorrow.

We soon discovered that there was in fact a new generation ready to take up the torch. Of the thirty or so designers and studios that we singled out at the time, twelve appear in this book. By what qualities were they selected? Above all, a personal voice and unique approach, as well as a distinctive way of conceiving interior design. Indeed, despite their wide stylistic diversity, whether minimalist or quasi-baroque, glamorous or architectural, the designers presented here share many points in common that combine to delineate a new French style. With elegance, aesthetic freedom, and sometimes audacity, they all uphold a kind of classicism (no one can completely sever their cultural roots) without ever losing sight of that elusive attribute called "chic." Cool and often unconventional, the new chic has adapted to modern-day tastes and lifestyles while drawing liberally from the heritage of the twentieth-century decorative arts, freely combining vintage furniture, creations by the interior designers themselves, gallery pieces, and, of course, contemporary artworks. Another of its hallmarks, and one that links this fresh vision of chic to the grand decorative traditions, is its reliance on the skills of exceptional artisans, one of France's proudest cultural assets.

After identifying the young contenders upon whom we were ready to wager, we followed and supported their work in the pages of our magazine. And we invited them to participate in the various editions of *AD Intérieurs*, an exhibition that we organize each year, giving a select group of interior designers carte blanche to create a living space on a given theme. The event, inspired by the Salon des Artistes Décorateurs, the showcase for the great talents of the twentieth century, offers them complete liberty of expression, without the conditions imposed by a commission from a client. Many of the photos in this book show how the designers have taken advantage of *AD Intérieurs* to explore new stylistic realms.

Those whom we were calling the "stars of tomorrow" just a few years ago are now the stars of today. Their styles are fully developed, their studios have expanded, and they have built up an ever-growing international clientele. Always on the go, from airport to airport, country to country, they are increasingly difficult to pin down. That's the price of success. But after all of the adventures that we have shared with them—feature stories, portraits, interviews, decors for *AD Intérieurs*—we now enjoy a close relationship. In the following pages we tell the story of these encounters, recounted in words and images by the journalists of *AD*.

Marie Kalt,
editor in chief of AD *magazine France*

He is the very embodiment of the new French style, steeped in a form of radicalized classicism. With his handsome face (he has been known to work as a model for luxury labels like Berluti) and typically Parisian laid-back look—jeans, sneakers, unruly hair—Joseph Dirand is quite the trendsetter. From his drawing board have come the decors for the most fashionable hotspots in Paris, like the restaurant Monsieur Bleu at the Palais de Tokyo, a balance between art deco opulence and 1950s modernism, or Loulou at the Louvre, a blend of belle epoque references and retro-futurism. "My work is a narrative—it tells stories," Dirand assures us. "The Eero Saarinen chair that I chose for Loulou is a good example: like a pair of Converse sneakers, it's part of our shared culture. It plays on the collective memory."

Far from being a hipster preoccupied with being cool, Dirand is above all an impressive stylist, skillfully mixing seemingly antithetical genres to compose ambiences that appear to exist outside of time. This Parisian, born in 1974 and a graduate of the Paris-Belleville Architecture School, first acquired a reputation for interiors—apartments, hotels, and shops—that draw on the graphic power of black and white. But with maturity he has evolved toward a softer-edged approach, with more room for fantasy. "I was always interested in minimalism, in strong, precise expression. Having pursued this vocabulary to the point of abstraction, in order to avoid repeating myself and maintain my level of excitement, I started to put more into my projects. They have become increasingly rich, increasingly complex, with more and more references."

His vision of a series of neoclassical reception rooms for the house of Balmain in 2009 led to a string of commissions from the big names in luxury. Since then he has delivered shops for Givenchy, Pucci, Chloé, and Rick Owens. Not wishing to be tied down to a single type of project, the French designer takes on wide-ranging missions, for example working simultaneously on a private island in the Bahamas, a skyscraper in Miami, and a restaurant in New York. While his high-profile projects continue to expand in scope, Dirand is also interested in the small scale, and is developing a limited-edition furniture collection. "I often use furniture by architects, like Oscar Niemeyer, in my interiors," he says. "With their spare lines, my radical proposals are in the same vein. I conceive my own pieces like miniature architectural structures." This minimalist approach harks back to his early interiors. But according to Dirand, "It's my way of going forward. In order to build, I must first lay the foundation. With time, I will no doubt take more liberty in the development of my furniture. What interests me most is doing things that I've never done before!"

Cédric Saint André Perrin

Joseph Dirand
Elegance
Made in France

Joseph Dirand in the "Utopian Dwelling Cell" that he created for *AD Intérieurs* 2011, with a video projection by Adrien Dirand as *a tableau vivant.*

This London apartment expresses Joseph Dirand's vision of minimalism, with an air of prestige: the marble-topped table by Hervé Van der Straeten, the armchairs by Pierre Jeanneret, and the chandelier by Paavo Tynell.

ABOVE AND OPPOSITE In this Parisian apartment, Joseph Dirand reinvents classicism with a virtuosic touch. The dining room is a harmony of spare modernism and traditional moldings, with a table and chairs of his own design under a pendant lamp by Hervé Van der Straeten. The decor for the kitchen creates a contrast between marble, crafted with modernist lines, and a two-level table surrounded by Warren Platner chairs. The pendant lamp is by Éric Schmitt.

PREVIOUS PAGES In London, the dazzling blue of a painting by Jean-Michel Basquiat brightens a living room in shades of gray and white. The coffee table is by Ado Chale, the armchairs by Pierre Jeanneret, and the long sofa by Christian Liaigre. | OPPOSITE AND ABOVE A Paris townhouse with a living room that opens onto a terrace. Around the copper coffee table, designed by Dirand, are an armchair and sofa by Pierre Jeanneret. The *Bells* pendant lamp is by Ronan and Erwan Bouroullec. The marble bathroom is decorated with a chair by Oscar Niemeyer and, to the right, an *LP10* sconce by Luigi Caccia Dominioni.

PREVIOUS PAGES In Paris, a black-and-white bedroom with an *Elda* armchair by Joe Colombo and a *Solaris* pedestal table by Martin Szekely. The painting above the bed is by Jonathan Binet. | ABOVE AND OPPOSITE White is the predominant color in the designer's own apartment in Paris. In the living room, the sofa and chairs are by Pierre Jeanneret, the coffee table by Ron Arad, and the stool by Le Corbusier. Above the fireplace is a painting by Lawrence Carroll. In the bedroom, the white suede chair was designed by Oscar Niemeyer.

Joseph Dirand's art deco–inspired "Maharajah's Bathroom" for *AD Intérieurs* 2012, in Calacatta marble with ebony woodwork and bronze trim.

OPPOSITE For this living room overlooking the Tuileries Garden, Joseph Dirand surrounded a travertine coffee table by Jean Prouvé with an *Ours Polaire* living room set by Jean Royère.
ABOVE Dirand counterbalanced the classicism of this Paris townhouse with a Pierre Jeanneret desk and an artwork by John Baldessari on the wall.

Slim, pointed shoes, a tight-fitting jacket, a loose shock of hair, a gleam in his eye, and a spring in his step . . . It's impossible to look at Vincent Darré without thinking of Jean Cocteau. Like the late French poet, filmmaker, and illustrator, the interior designer is a well-known figure in Parisian society. No charity gala, exhibition opening, or fashion event would be complete without his effervescent presence. "Everyone thinks I'm some kind of gadabout or party animal, but actually I'm just a big neurotic," he admits. "I'd much rather spend an evening at the theater than at a fragrance launch."

And just like Cocteau, Darré is a multitalented artist, by turns a designer of interiors, fashion, and stage costumes, an illustrator, and even a sometime fashion photographer. "When I was younger I wanted to create film and theater sets," he recounts. "I enrolled at the École des Arts Décoratifs, but then I got caught up in the scene at the Palace [the famous Paris nightclub of the late 1970s]. With so many parties to go to, I found myself piecing together clothes for my girlfriends and, following that thread, I ended up working in fashion. Then again, fashion at the time was very theatrical!" As an assistant to Yves Saint Laurent, a stylist in Italy, and a longtime collaborator of Karl Lagerfeld's, Darré earned his stripes in the garment trade before returning to his first love in 2008. "An exhibition on Dadaism at the Centre Pompidou was the turning point. I had just finished a stint with Ungaro, which frankly didn't work out well at all. I was really unhappy, and then suddenly, seeing those artworks, I realized that I had taken a wrong turn in my life. Deep down, what I like are collages, eye-catching things with lots of energy. I had been trying like crazy to become the creative director of a major label, but it just wasn't right for me. I needed to express myself more freely, and furniture seemed to be the right medium."

There followed the tables with skeletal legs or painting-like tops, the bizarre lobster cabinets . . . "I have often been hastily labeled a 'surrealist,' but

Vincent Darré
Chic Fantasies

my influences are more complex than that," the designer explains. "I adore a certain grand French decorative style *à la* Jansen, the English spirit of David Hicks . . . I'm also very much inspired by the Italian baroque. Then I put it all together in my own mishmash!"

In addition to furniture, Darré creates spaces—often, not surprisingly, festive ones, like the Montana nightclub in Paris's Saint-Germain district, and its hotel consisting entirely of theme-based suites. Also decors for special events, operas, and films, and private residences as well. His most recent project is a showroom apartment on the Right Bank that features his own furniture plus carefully chosen antiques, tableware, wallpaper . . . "Everything is for sale!" he says. "The idea is to create a new decor every season, just like in fashion. That's where I came from, and old habits die hard."

Cédric Saint André Perrin

Vincent Darré at home, on a Napoléon III bed that he had upholstered with 1970s-style fabrics. Above the headboard is a surgeon's lamp from the 1920s.

The designer's home in Paris. All in vivid colors, a chair by Warren Platner accompanies a vintage bench, a red Venetian sofa, and Vincent Darré's own *Bassin* coffee table.

OPPOSITE AND ABOVE The Spanish model Inés Sastre's pied-à-terre in Paris. Red reigns supreme, with wallpaper and a rug designed by Darré in the hallway and, in the kitchen, a vintage feel with a 1960s Finnish table, plus chairs and a wall-mounted screen from the 1950s. The pendant lamp, also vintage, is by Jacques Biny.

ABOVE AND OPPOSITE In Inés Sastre's Paris apartment, the blue decor of the bedroom evokes a Hollywood-style boudoir. To the right of the bed, the *Grenouille* nightstand is a Vincent Darré creation. The wall covering was designed by Pierre Le-Tan and the armchair and ottoman are upholstered with fabric from the 1940s.

OPPOSITE AND ABOVE A Parisian apartment decorated in a medley of colors and patterns. In the living room, two *Écrevisse* storage columns frame the doorway, against a backdrop of *Métamorph'Os* wallpaper, all creations by Maison Darré. Across the room, also by Vincent Darré, a *Fait-Mur* mirror joins a sofa, cushions from the *Ossobucco* collection, and a *Bassin* table.

ABOVE Vincent Darré has turned his bedroom into a veritable curiosity shop, with an armchair inherited from his grandmother, his *Échasse* console table, bell jars, a 1950s tapestry, a baroque mirror . . . | OPPOSITE For this three-level apartment in Paris, Darré created a dining room with a 1950s feel, exemplified by the tapestry and the choice of ceramics.

The "Dadaist Boudoir" presented at *AD Intérieurs* 2012. The space centers around the *Métaphysique* screen, designed by Vincent Darré, like the sofa, occasional table, and rug. The chair on the right is by Jean Royère and the blue pendant lamp by Roberto Menghi.

OPPOSITE The "Little Prince Bedroom" created for the 2013 edition of *AD Intérieurs*—in Vincent Darré's own words, "An overdose of prints!" For the occasion, he decorated his furniture designs with fabric patterns from the Pierre Frey archives. The *Hirondelles* chandelier is by Aristide Najean. | ABOVE Darré's "Acid Blue" suite at the chic and ultra-eccentric Hôtel Montana in Paris. The furniture and decorative objects were collected by the designer.

ABOVE A detail of the wallpaper in Vincent Darré's home, a creation by Maison Darré, like the triangular *Méphisto* box. | OPPOSITE Ensconced in the designer's living room, underneath a painting by Gérard Garouste, is an eighteenth-century sofa. On the *Arêtes* rug are two *Pas Gigogne* coffee tables, all creations by Maison Darré.

When people ask Jean-Louis Deniot how he developed such a passion for his profession, he says he doesn't know. He recalls that as a young boy he used to draw floorplans in chalk on the pavement of parking lots, and liked to build model homes. But school bored him, much to his parents' dismay. For two years he took drafting classes offered by the city of Paris before convincing them to let him enroll at the École Camondo. At last he had found his element, and he graduated in June 2000.

Two months later he opened his studio and began decorating apartments offered for sale by an American company and local real estate agents. In addition to the ultra-contemporary style favored at Camondo, Deniot also felt the need to learn from friends like Alexandre Pradère, an expert in antique furniture who taught him the French classical style. Pradère says of him, "He's very talented! He was already a virtuoso at Camondo and he has lived up to his promise, with an eclectic sense of taste and a solid knowledge of classical architecture and decoration—plus genuine human qualities and an incredible energy for juggling projects on several continents."

Deniot was soon an international success. Foreign clients who liked his work on their Parisian pieds-à-terre asked him to refurbish their primary residences in their home countries, especially the United States, where his interiors have appeared on the covers of the major decorating magazines. How does he describe his style? "It evolves every day. I have no standard materials. I'm interested in variety, in the juxtaposition of different finishes. I work with French craftsmen: painters, decorators, specialists in painting on silk or gilt glass, cord and tassel makers, locksmiths ... I encourage them to adapt their artisanal techniques to the more informal tastes of today. Each project is very different, intrinsically linked to a site, a country. The floorplan is a key element: there's a logic to each structure and each lifestyle. Very often I need to rethink the entire space." To do that, Deniot closes his eyes and imagines himself in the rooms, seeing the lines, the light, the colors. It's no wonder he's always jotting down notes on his cell phone, no matter where he is.

"A house follows a chronology," he says. "Each piece of furniture and each finishing has its degree of importance. You can't show everything right at

Jean-Louis Deniot
Material Eloquence

the entrance—there has to be a gradual progression. The dining room, or even more so the dining room-kitchen, if they're combined in one space, must be the most sophisticated, because it's the most festive room in the house."

Composing with textures, mixing materials, asking a woman who creates knits for haute couture houses to make a braided leather ornament, noting the shape of a doorknob or a round Anglo-Chinese table spotted at a friend's apartment . . . Such is Deniot's everyday routine. People wonder how he can remain so calm while completing a hotel in Paris, an entire skyscraper in Miami, plus a string of private homes around the world. At least part of his secret: regular Pilates sessions.

Aude de La Conté

Jean-Louis Deniot in the decor that he created for the 2011 *AD Intérieurs* exhibition.

A Parisian living room conceived as an homage to Jean-Michel Frank. Jean-Louis Deniot designed the straw marquetry coffee table and the "jewel" mirror above the mica-encrusted fireplace. The sofas, dating from 1950, are flanked by cement and metal lamps by Mathilde Pénicaud.

ABOVE AND OPPOSITE For this 1930s Hollywood residence by the architect Paul R. Williams, Jean-Louis Deniot has preserved the original New Regency style, enhancing it here at the foot of the staircase, with a red lacquer desk from Maison Jansen, a resin stool by Claudio Salocchi (circa 1970), and a chandelier by Curtis Jere. The dining room combines a white leather-lined table with Kipp Stewart chairs from the 1960s and an eighteenth-century Swedish portrait.

OPPOSITE Decked out in silvery linen, this Paris dining room features a made-to-measure mahogany table surrounded by Danish-style chairs by Franco Campo and Carlo Graffi. The bronze chandelier is by Hervé Van der Straeten. | ABOVE The entrance to this classic nineteenth-century Parisian apartment conveys timeless elegance with a stainless steel sculpture by Edgard Pillet in the background, a console from the 1980s, and gleaming lacquered doors.

PREVIOUS PAGES For the 2012 *AD Intérieurs* exhibition, Jean-Louis Deniot dreamed up this ethnic-graphic living room draped in wild silk and equipped with an imposing brass and parchment chandelier of his own design. | ABOVE AND OPPOSITE Refined opulence in a small Parisian apartment. The kitchen is decorated with sumptuous materials like marble and hammered silver panels. The chandelier is a vintage Stilnovo creation. In the dining room, the table by Roger Thibier is paired with Jacques Adnet chairs created for UNESCO.

OPPOSITE In this Parisian "railroad" apartment, the kitchen-dining room is decorated with a made-to-measure Danish-style table and chairs upholstered with horsehair. | ABOVE This bedroom in Paris is lined with imitation parchment panels. In front of the bed, two Ramos armchairs flank a Gio Ponti coffee table holding ceramic pieces and a lamp by Kéramos.

PREVIOUS PAGES The living room of this vacation home in Corsica opens onto the patio. Jean-Louis Deniot created the rug and coffee tables. The sofas are by Vladimir Kagan and the chandelier by Oswald Haerdtl. On the left is a sculptural floor lamp by Charles Trevelyan, and on the right a Pierre Paulin armchair with its ottoman. | ABOVE AND OPPOSITE In Capri, Jean-Louis Deniot composed a decor with a vintage feel for this vacation home in a former presbytery. The vintage spirit carries over to the entrance and staircase in the subtle curves of the masonry. The dining room houses an Italian chandelier from the 1960s and a Jacques Jarrige table. The large-format photograph on the wall is *Spanish Bath* by James Casebere.

Already as students at Penninghen, Laurent Buttazzoni and Frédéric Lavaud admired the same references in architecture and contemporary art—and shared the same relative lack of admiration for the Memphis Group, whose convoluted motifs were then all the rage, to the point of being branded minimalists. Early experience with Andrée Putman tempered their stance somewhat: "There were all kinds of projects," they recall. "It was the era of 3 Suisses [the mail order house] and so forth. The designs were carefully worked out, very exacting but also decorative. Everything had to be graphically appealing." Buttazzoni was the first to go solo, in 1995, before Lavaud officially became his associate ten years later.

Meanwhile, a constant emerged in their projects: color, rarely primary and tinged with a 1970s inspiration. Their interiors always demonstrate a striking color sense, expressed in the upholstery of an armchair or the palette of a photograph hung on the wall, shattering the disciplined reserve of the white box. "The use of color buttresses the architecture" the partners say, "like a counterweight to its strictness. 'Strict': the definition can apply to us, as long as it goes hand-in-hand with a certain lightness. After all, you have to have a sense of fun to produce a pleasant space!" Their impeccable volumes are punctuated with a few bright touches, even mixing periods and styles, without losing sight of their decidedly contemporary essence.

In every direction, white reigns by contrast, revealing the precision of the lines and the balance of proportions, in order to accentuate the project's highly architectural approach and silence any trace of vain grandiloquence.

The galleries were immediately won over, and the agency was commissioned to design "white cubes" for Kreo, Thaddaeus Ropac, etc. Quite naturally, the collectors followed: "Everything takes off from the drawing, of course. Then, once the box looks good you can put whatever you want in it . . . We're rather eclectic when it comes to furniture, since we have to compose the space with the collector's artworks in mind, and know how to arrange them. In relation to an artwork, we try to stay in the background

Buttazzoni & Associés
Pop-Tinged Precision

and make it the center of attention—we're not the artists." Thus, paintings and sculptures have played an increasingly prominent role in the projects by Buttazzoni & Associés, becoming centerpieces that the designers have learned to use as leverage points, bringing out their qualities and intuiting their decorative value. With their distinctive visual power, they impose their presence in the space, guaranteeing the air of creative flamboyance that always characterizes a Buttazzoni and Lavaud interior. Like a guardrail that prevents them from straying into the realm of decorative overload—the "pastiche revival" that they make every effort to avoid.

Oscar Duboÿ

Laurent Buttazzoni and Frédéric Lavaud in their *"Midnight Blue Bachelor's Apartment"* created for the 2010 edition of *AD Intérieurs.*

A pop spirit for the living room of a country house all in wood. In front of the *Amphis* sofa by Pierre Paulin are a Martin Szekely occasional table and the *Nuage* coffee table by Guy de Rougemont. The artworks on the wall are *BJ'S* by Jack Pierson and two paintings by Peter Zimmermann.

OPPOSITE A contemporary country house. The hanging sculpture is by Éric Duyckaerts, the coffee table by Martin Szekely, the floor lamp by Gino Sarfatti, and the mirror by Pierre Charpin. | ABOVE White walls but a colorful decor for this lounge area in a house in Sicily, with a yellow USM sideboard, two gilded lamps, and vintage ceramics.

ABOVE For this classic Parisian apartment, Laurent Buttazzoni and Frédéric Lavaud composed a spare decor in delicate colors. In the dining room, a circular work by the artist Blair Thurman, *Dawn Patrol*, dialogues with a tiled bench by Aldo Cibic. | OPPOSITE In the living room, two Wolfgang Brengenzer coffee tables are surrounded by a Hans J. Wegner armchair, a mosaic table by Pierre Charpin, and paintings by Davide Balula and Camille Henrot.

PREVIOUS PAGES For this traditional Sicilian house, Laurent Buttazzoni created a staircase inspired by a Japanese furniture design, conceived to save space in order to maximize the fireplace area. A *Vidun* coffee table by Vico Magistretti is surrounded by Harry Bertoia chairs, with a Jean Prouvé bench in the background. | OPPOSITE A lounge area in a Parisian apartment with the square as a recurring theme, from the photograph to the marble fireplace. On the floor to the right is a *Cesta* lamp by Miguel Milá. | ABOVE In the architectural kitchen of this country house, the Corian and stainless-steel counter-table and the stools were designed by Laurent Buttazzoni and Frédéric Lavaud. The chandelier is by Jeff Zimmerman.

PREVIOUS PAGES Laurent Buttazzoni's living room in Paris is a study in symmetry: the two red doors, each crowned with a contemporary artwork, frame a painting by Marc Quinn. Buttazzoni designed the sofa-bed and coffee table. | ABOVE A lounge area in a Parisian residence. A colorful textile sculpture by Sheila Hicks contrasts with an ivory sofa by Pierre Paulin and a rug designed by Buttazzoni & Associés. The lamp is by Gino Sarfatti.

ABOVE A graphic minimalist look for the dining room of a Parisian apartment, with the *Roches* shelves by the Bouroullec brothers and a collection of ceramics and bronzes.

ABOVE The dining room of Buttazzoni's Paris apartment, bathed in midnight blue. And, as always, light touches of contrasting color. | OPPOSITE This small bedroom in a house in Sicily is decorated with an interplay of lines that seems to enlarge the space. Buttazzoni's emblematic red adds graphic accents. A dressing area is concealed behind the dramatic headboard.

To paraphrase Brillat-Savarin, "Tell me where you work and I will tell you who you are." A visit to the spacious Haussmann-style apartment that serves as headquarters for Dorothée Boissier and Patrick Gilles gives an immediate insight into their style. Nothing over the top, with color choices that interlink and interact, a spectrum of grays and beiges across a palette of precious materials. Here and there, a few more monumental pieces to energize this placid electrocardiogram of a decor: a bust, a broad decorative bamboo screen . . . There is no lack of clever twists, but they remain details rather than highlights, like the gray fur bristling from Boissier's armchair as she describes their process: "More than the decoration, we work on the volumes. How is the space used over time? How will the occupants experience it? Everything else proceeds from that, including the choice of a chair—if we put it in a certain place, it's because it has a specific role to play there in relation to the layout. You can create a beautiful decor, but if the proportions and the floorplan are wrong, it's going to be a disaster." An interior by Gilles & Boissier is always painstakingly structured, the space finely calibrated by hand—literally: there is no sign of a computer in Gilles's office.

And then what? How do they soften the overall effect? Little by little, the two designers found their formula, drawing on sources of inspiration far from the world of interiors: "We often tackle a project with one principle in mind: everything but the decor. It can range from dance to film, a book, an artist . . . In any case, always with a human focus. In one instance it was a scene from a ballet by Sylvie Guillem with Akram Khan—a sublime image that stayed with us, and the rest fell into place like a puzzle." The "rest" might include, for example, asking the landscape artist and engraver François Houtin to create an enveloping mural of a forest to enliven the small space of Caffè Artcurial.

Like the artists Cyprien Chabert and Alix Waline, Houtin is one of the designers' regular collaborators, and the creator of another large fresco

Gilles & Boissier
Classic & Cool

for the Moncler flagship on rue du Faubourg Saint-Honoré—one of many projects that have united Gilles & Boissier with Remo Ruffini, CEO of the famous down jacket label. The partners excel at this type of stylistic exercise, tempering the extravagance of a brand image with a French-style elegance that doesn't seek simply to dazzle, reflecting their early experience with Christian Liaigre and, for Boissier, Philippe Starck. Still today, those influences are very much present, allowing the duo to develop their understated aesthetic in projects like the Baccarat Hotel in New York City. "When they hired us, Starwood [the hotel's owners] knew that we would avoid any kind of 'Las Vegas' look, and that the end result would be calm and soothing," Boissier recounts. "But ultimately, that encouraged us to push the envelope!" Going further but never too far—just to the limits of a refined harmony.

Oscar Duboÿ

Dorothée Boissier and Patrick Gilles in a villa on the Basque coast that they have refurbished. Behind them, a painting by the contemporary Italian painter Piero Pizzi Cannella.

Gilles & Boissier wanted to preserve the original dark woodwork of this villa in Biarritz. All of the furniture was designed by the two partners, including the black metal *Nestor* end table and the ceramic stools created for Christian Liaigre.

ABOVE The dining room of the Biarritz villa features a cedar table and white leather chairs by Gilles & Boissier under a Murano chandelier. | OPPOSITE For *AD Intérieurs* 2014, Gilles & Boissier created an all-wooden office installed around a small house, like a refuge to protect the occupants' intimacy while merging with the surroundings.

OPPOSITE The top-floor master bedroom of a house on the shores of Lake Como owned by Remo Ruffini, director of the Moncler fashion label. Here again, all of the furniture was designed by Gilles & Boissier, in dark wood enlivened with red accents. Above the bed is a copy of a Rubens painting. | ABOVE In the main sitting room of a Milanese apartment, black Marquina marble contrasts with a photograph taken by Robert Polidori at the Palace of Versailles.

In a corner of the living room of the partners' Paris apartment, a black spruce table is surrounded by a sofa and chairs in stained oak. The chair backs are upholstered with a fabric from the 1950s.

ABOVE The designers' bedroom in Paris. A peaceful, classically inspired setting that heightens the presence of two works by Christian Astuguevieille: the black hemp display case on the mantle and the vase on the table. | OPPOSITE This Milanese bathroom is decorated entirely in Calacatta Breccia marble. Except for the two nineteenth-century sconces, everything from the sink to the towel holder, mirror frame, and oak pendant lamp was designed by Gilles & Boissier.

OPPOSITE AND ABOVE Dorothée Gilles and Patrick Boissier designed all of the furniture for their Paris apartment. On the left, the cloth totem in the living room is by Christian Astuguevieille. In the hallway, a photo by Nadav Kandar sits on a table with a brushed oak underframe. The *Plein Soleil* pendant lamp was created by Gilles & Boissier for Pouenat.

OPPOSITE Black and white is a recurring theme in the decor of Remo Ruffini's house on Lake Como. All of the floors on the ground level feature a checkerboard motif. The sofa and footstools are Gilles & Boissier creations. | ABOVE A fresco by Mathias Kiss, modeled after a work in a Tuscan baroque church, adorns the gallery with its thematic two-tone tiled floor.

ABOVE In Gilles and Boissier's Paris apartment, a large-format painting by Christian Astuguevieille creates visual tension with the original moldings. The pumice stone table and ceramic stool were designed by the duo. | OPPOSITE L'Autre Appartement, an annex to the partners' agency in Paris that serves as a laboratory and a display space for their creations. Under the ceiling, with its vivid swathes of golden yellow, is a fresco by the artist Cyprien Chabert.

The first thing to strike the eye is his approach to materials. "I use light to bring out their opulence, their sophistication, their depth," Chahan Minassian explains. He uses a broad sensory palette, combining ceramics, linen, quartz, bronze, rope, and exotic woods in monochromatic ambiences. And through it all wafts a sort of gentle bluish breeze, a blue whose spectrum changes with the light to reveal other shades, from mossy gray-green to pale seashell pink. "In the gardens of Lebanon, where I grew up, you can often find little antique bronzes or glass lachrymatory vases. The quality of their iridescence and oxidized surfaces made a deep impression on me." His Lebanese childhood overlaid with Armenian culture no doubt also explains his taste for mixes and blends. "There was a remarkable concentration of influences in Lebanon in the 1960s. The East of course, but also the classical French decorative arts, because many homes had a 'French salon.' Then we discovered the American 'lifestyle' on television. And there was also the 1930s furniture—my grandparents' home was furnished in that style." He likes to describe his interiors as "timeless capsules." To create a moment suspended in time, he starts with the architecture of the space: "It's the shell that will house my textures, my materials, followed by the furniture and objets d'art that I'm constantly collecting. I choose the ones that I know will allow me to express myself. My perception captures them like a prism. They are my spices." Like an Ayurvedic doctor, he doses his ingredients differently for each client. In Paris, New York, or a site in Switzerland, from apartments to yachts, from country houses to executive offices, he punctuates his interiors with sculptural American furniture from the 1940s, '50s, and '60s, spectacular decorative objects and works by the artists whom he features in his gallery. Like Peter Lane, whose ceramics are characterized by the rich texture of their crazed surfaces, or Nancy Lorenz, a creator of precious lacquerware that integrates gold and silver.

Chahan Minassian is very attached to the concepts of commissions, bespoke work, and haute couture. Which is one of the reasons why he lives and works in Paris. "There are artisanal skills here that can't be found anywhere else. For twenty-five years I have been faithful to my suppliers, a handful of craftsmen who are ready to work twenty hours a day to give me what I need." Paris inspires him, and he inspires Paris. The majority of the projects that have captivated him the most over the past five years have been in the capital, including a pied-à-terre on the Esplanade des Invalides, a "Presidential Office" created for the 2014 edition of the *AD Intérieurs* exhibition at the Musée des Arts Décoratifs, and, of course, his interiors for the new Hôtel de Crillon, reopening in 2017. The luxury hotel on the place de la Concorde, once a palace for Queen Marie Antoinette, is also linked to the designer's past. "When I was a child," he recounts, "at a family reunion in the Crillon winter garden, I predicted to my mother that I would decorate the place one day. I believe in that kind of 'ricochet' of fate."

Axelle Corty

Chahan Minassian
Sumptuous Serenity

Chahan Minassian at home. The large sculpture is by Harry Bertoia. On the wall are a sconce by Max Ingrand and a cubist artwork by Carmelo Arden Quin. The coffee table is by Raphaël and the armchairs by Frank Lloyd Wright.

The "Presidential Office" presented at *AD Intérieurs* 2014, all in bronze, gold, and silver. Behind the desk by the sculptor César hangs a sculpture by Harry Bertoia. The sofas are by Vladimir Kagan and the coffee tables by Silas Seandel and Armand Jonckers.

OPPOSITE In this nineteenth-century Parisian apartment updated in a Venetian spirit, the small living room lined with Cordoba leather features a painting by Jean Renut, a neoclassical-style sofa from the 1940s, and a Murano glass floor lamp. On the coffee table is a bronze case by Paul Evans. | ABOVE The sequence of rooms unfolds like a fanciful tableau of Venice, with shades of blue to evoke the lagoon, lots of velvet and brocades, eighteenth-century pieces, and antiqued mirrors. | FOLLOWING PAGES In a palette of powdery grays, this nineteenth-century Parisian living room features a harmonious blend of styles: two armchairs from the eighteenth and nineteenth centuries, a méridienne in a 1940s spirit designed by Minassian, a trio of *Nuage* coffee tables by Kam Tin, and, on the left, a gilded painting by Nancy Lorenz, one of the artists represented by Chahan Gallery.

ABOVE For the decor of this Paris apartment from the 1950s, Chahan Minassian focused on wood and plants. In the bedroom, with its gold raffia walls, a mirror sculpture by an anonymous artist dominates the bed. On the floor is a copper *FedEx Box* by Walead Beshty. | OPPOSITE In a corner of the living room, with its eighteenth-century woodwork, a papier-mâché sculpture by Franz West sits on a graceful desk by a student of Gio Ponti. The Plexiglas armchair is unsigned and the rug was made to measure by David Hicks.

The "Californian Living Room" created for the 2012 *AD Intérieurs* exhibition. With a palette based on subtle variations of ivory, a Chahan Minassian signature, the decor juxtaposes a ceramic wall by Peter Lane with a Vladimir Kagan sofa, under the gaze of a Bernard Buffet painting.

OPPOSITE In this living room conceived for *AD Intérieurs* 2011, Chahan Minassian created a daring clash of styles and periods with *Rhythm*, an installation by Arne Quinze crafted from recuperated fence boards (2011) interacting with the original nineteenth-century molding, and a shimmering, mirror-like floor. | ABOVE The long table in wood, steel, and bronze was designed by Minassian. Surrounded by Paul Evans chairs, it holds two mercury silvered glass sculptures by Ritsue Mishima and, in the back, a sculpture by Johan Creten entitled *Les Poulpes*. The two chandeliers are Venini creations from the 1960s. | FOLLOWING PAGES The living room of Chahan Minassian's apartment centers around the fireplace, decorated with ceramics by Peter Lane. The painting above it is by Richard Serra, and on the left is *1%*, an artwork in resin by Aaron Young. A sofa by Federico Munari and two armchairs by T. H. Robsjohn-Gibbings encircle an *Eternal Forest* coffee table by Philip and Kelvin LaVerne. In the foreground is an *Orque* chair by Jean-Philippe Gleizes.

ABOVE A detail of a brass and coral sculpture-desk attributed to Jacques Duval-Brasseur in the guestroom of Minassian's apartment. | OPPOSITE *Scholar Rocks*, a diptych by Nancy Lorenz, adorns the lounge area. Chahan Minassian designed the sofa, accompanied on the right by a Philippe Hiquily pedestal table and a nest of tables by Jacques Adnet. The coffee table in the middle is by Paul Evans, who also designed the pedestal table in the foreground, alongside an *Erica* chaise longue by Vladimir Kagan.

These days I want color!" The statement sounds like a challenge coming from Pierre Yovanovitch, a designer known for his serene interiors in low-key tones of white, beige, and blond wood. We are visiting one of his latest worksites, a spacious townhouse whose walls are still white with primer: five levels of sumptuous luxury, with carefully laid-out volumes and lines that intertwine, like the sculptural central staircase, joining in a dialogue from one floor to the next. This is what Yovanovitch likes best: to conceive a living space based on the elemental structure of a building, recreating every room to enhance the lives of its occupants. As always, he will create a highly architectural interior that emanates comfort and refinement. He will sketch out the key pieces of furniture and most exacting installations, custom dressing rooms, and personalized bathrooms. The difference here will be the advent of color. Peacock blue for the woodwork of a sitting room, Chinese red walls, and a gilded ceiling for a bar . . . One can imagine the visual impact.

After earning a degree in business administration, Yovanovitch first worked for Pierre Cardin before deciding to make a living doing what he loved most: decorating homes. He started with his own, using a succession of apartments as both a creative laboratory and a funding source; he sold each one after completing its renovation. Then he began working for friends, and finally for clients with the opening of his agency in 2000. "I feel free," the designer says when asked about his career. "I've read a lot, especially on the decorative arts, to make up for my lack of formal study. On the other hand, since I didn't have a specific taste imposed by teachers, I forged my own." A process that culminated in 2006 with a milestone exhibition, *Swedish Grace*, that he hosted at his home, in collaboration with the antiques dealer Eric Philippe. "I wanted to highlight the Scandinavian style that I find so moving," Yovanovitch explains. "But I'm also drawn to the creations of today's designers." Like Matali Crasset, from whom he commissioned three lamps for a townhouse.

The designer also has a passion for contemporary art. To his great satisfaction, the opulent homes that he furnishes provide opportunities to meet and work with the most illustrious artists. "That's the fun part of my work," he says with a smile. This tall, handsome man seems perfectly calm on the outside, but inside he is constantly preoccupied—with ideas, projects, reflections . . .

Pierre Yovanovitch
Pared-Down Poetry

His Paris-based agency (which he recently moved to a more central location) is expanding fast, and the commissions keep coming, especially from the United States, where he plans to open an office in 2017. At age fifty, Pierre Yovanovitch is buoyed by his success, but while he admits to being ambitious, he is well aware of the stakes: "This development in the U.S. is a big step for the company." But we can rest assured that his talent will carry him through. Meanwhile, he's taking two days off to do some gardening at his castle in southern France, surrounded by his beloved dogs.

Marion Bley

Pierre Yovanovitch in the Scandinavian-inspired space that he created for *AD Intérieurs* in 2010. The sculpture to his left is by Stephan Balkenhol.

For this Parisian living room, Pierre Yovanovitch dreamed up a spectacular ceiling with backlit cutouts. He also created the sofa that winds around an Edward Wormley coffee table, a vintage American chair, tufted chairs by Billy Haines, and photographs by Nobuyoshi Araki.

ABOVE AND OPPOSITE Pierre Yovanovitch gave the entrance of this Parisian townhouse a strikingly graphic look. The red-and-black lacquered sideboard by Paul Laszlo holds ceramics by Dani and Jacques Ruelland. The photographs are by Maïko Haruki. The black-and-white marble floor reflects the wrought-iron door, designed by Yovanovitch.

OPPOSITE For a Parisian residence, Pierre Yovanovitch designed this spiral staircase to serve as the centerpiece of the decor. | ABOVE Seen at *AD Intérieurs* 2011, this alcove living room was conceived as a space for contemplation in which to watch a video by the artist Bill Viola. | FOLLOWING PAGES The living room of Pierre Yovanovitch's castle in Provence. Everything has been redesigned and recreated, down to the beams and fireplace. The sofas are by Yovanovitch, the two chairs by Otto Schultz, and the *Mesa Coffee Table* by T. H. Robsjohn-Gibbings.

ABOVE This long, narrow kitchen in Paris features a black granite counter. The globular pendant lamps are by Nendo and the photograph on the wall is by Sam Samore. | OPPOSITE For the same apartment, Pierre Yovanovitch created a massive, majestic headboard in sanded oak, defying the reduced proportions of the bedroom.

OPPOSITE For this chalet in Switzerland, Pierre Yovanovitch upheld Alpine tradition by putting the spotlight on wood. The table and chairs are his own designs, the chandelier is by Studio Drift, and the lantern by Matali Crasset. | ABOVE Adjoining the dining room, under the staircase, are a statue by Ugo Rondinone and a small bench by Yovanovitch. | FOLLOWING PAGES In this chalet in Andermatt, the sofa, one of Yovanovitch's own creations, spans the entire living room. To the left of the staircase are chairs by Roberto Matta, and the fireplace to the right is equipped with a ceramic hood by Armelle Benoit. The two-level coffee table was made to measure by the designer and sculptor Matthias Kohn.

ABOVE Pierre Yovanovitch's bedroom in Provence. The raw wood bed is his own design, produced by his partner Pierre-Éloi Bris. The spherical cushions are one of his signature touches. The floor lamp in the background is by Gabriella Crespi, circa 1960. | OPPOSITE The Scandinavian-tinged dining room of Yovanovitch's Provençal castle. Above the sideboard by Christen Emanuel Kjær Monberg, dating from 1923, is a painted bas-relief portrait by Stephan Balkenhol. The chandelier is the work of Paavo Tynell, circa 1945.

Despite his impeccable credentials in interior design, including a degree from Penninghen in 1996 and experience with both Christian Liaigre and Philippe Starck, Tristan Auer's interests extend beyond decors: he also loves beautiful cars. He has even worked with automakers, refining that small intimate space in front of the steering wheel, where he feels right at home. And it's not just a trivial sideline—on the contrary, that same impetus is what gives his interiors their decidedly masculine quality, their powerful, head-on style, whether for a Left Bank townhouse or a villa on Mustique Island for the pop singer Bryan Adams. And, like a professional driver, he's always trying to outdo himself, even to the point of near-recklessness, letting no dark corner or ill-placed beam stand in the way of his vision.

creative outpouring that the Auer style is revealed, in his decorative research more than in a specific palette or recurrent vocabulary. He sees each commission as a new challenge to be met, formulating a made-to-measure response. "There's that feeling, both laborious and nearly euphoric, of finding the solution after a long time spent looking, and then being able to move on. Actually, I might have liked being a fashion designer, starting over

Tristan Auer
Rigorous Refinement

"I think I'm better when I have restrictions," he says. "I like the idea of venturing out of my comfort zone, because deep down we do our best work when we're trying something we've never done before."

Indeed, Auer is always willing to try something daring—like the sculptural neon lamps in the dressing room that he dreamed up for the 2014 *AD Intérieurs* exhibition at the Musée des Arts Décoratifs, creating a harmony of vivid shades and muted tones. Each project is an idea incubator, always including a "purification" phase to eliminate any superfluous details. His monumental but deconstructed decors for the Cartier jewelry brand at the Biennale des Antiquaires, his monastic-futuristic stand for the silversmith Puiforcat at the Maison et Objet fair . . . It's in this

completely every season, or a set designer—those situations in which you have to lose yourself in order to stick to a story," the designer suggests by way of describing the compelling atmosphere that permeates his interiors, especially the hotels that he renovates. Exoticism at the Cotton House in the Caribbean, contemporary eclecticism at La Sivolière in the Alpine resort of Courchevel . . . Each site corresponds to a theme that Auer depicts, making lavish use of unusual colors and equally imaginative materials. Interiors that express a strong identity, but never neglect comfort. "After all, isn't the purpose of interior design to make people happy?" he asks. "It may seem like a cliché, but I want to make genuine living spaces, and not cold representations."

Oscar Duboÿ

Tristan Auer at the 2014 AD Intérieurs exhibition, for which he created a "Dandy's Dressing Room."

In this Parisian apartment overlooking Les Invalides, Pierre Paulin chairs dialogue with a sofa by Vladimir Kagan. Between them is a coffee table by Max Ingrand, and on the wall to the right a stained glass mosaic by Valentin Carron.

OPPOSITE AND ABOVE Les Bains, the legendary Paris nightclub now converted into a high-luxury hotel and restaurant. Tristan Auer conceived the decors of its forty rooms, including a palatial suite, as well as the exotic, mysterious ambience of this "Chinese Lounge."

ABOVE Tristan Auer's "Dandy's Studio" for *AD Intérieurs* 2010 juxtaposed a spare graphic setting with a strapped-down daybed in front of a screen. The red wall and the Italian painting by Fra' Galgario add a tinge of flamboyant classicism. | OPPOSITE At *AD Intérieurs* 2014, Tristan Auer presented a dressing room composed of small, ultra-refined alcoves, like so many individual installations. A precious detail: the small shelf adorned with stained wood and bone marquetry. | FOLLOWING PAGES Against the white background of the living room of this Parisian apartment, the elegant gray monochrome of the sofa on the left—by Christophe Delcourt, who also created the ceramic coffee table on the right—provides a counterpoint to a vintage sofa and a rug designed by Auer. The high shelf unit is made of travertine and the fireplace is adorned with a sculpted metallized wood panel by Georges Muquet.

OPPOSITE Three eye-catching creations enhance the decor of this Left Bank townhouse: a coffee table by Barber & Osgerby, an Amanda Levete bench, and a side table-lamp by the Bouroullec brothers. | ABOVE This Parisian living room space is decorated with an antique sideboard found in Antwerp, a Pouenat end table, and a Florence Knoll chair.

ABOVE AND OPPOSITE The countertop of this kitchen, for *AD Intérieurs* 2011, is a bronze island facing a sculpture by Douglas White. Tristan Auer created the space for aesthetes rather than chefs, adorning it with artworks like a fragmented fresco by Rupert Shrive, along with a translucent *Presenze* chair by Nucleo. The table was designed by Auer himself.

OPPOSITE AND ABOVE The "Garçonnière en Grisaille" (bachelor's apartment in shades of gray) installed at the Hôtel de la Monnaie for *AD Intérieurs* 2016. In this precious, masculine space, the metal of the structure and the sculptures by Michel Anasse echo the colors of the frescoes, the fabric on the wall, a lacquer piece by Anne Midavaine, and a sofa by Tristan Auer.

ABOVE AND OPPOSITE The kitchen and living room of the Paris apartment of an American collector. In the kitchen, under the *Lianes* pendant lamp by Erwan and Ronan Bouroullec, is a rough-hewn table by Dominique Zimbacca surrounded by *Metropolitan* chairs. On the wall is a video painting by the Turkish artist Kutlug Ataman. The living room features a Pierre Paulin *Élysée* sofa, a Jean Royère coffee table, and, over the fireplace, a hanging sculpture by Michel François.

An architect, interior designer, furniture designer, and decorator, India Mahdavi originally dreamed of becoming a filmmaker. But she ended up studying architecture, graphics, and furniture design in Paris and later in New York. A decision that she doesn't regret: "My work is similar to that of a film director," explains this fan of Lang, Kubrick, Fellini, and Visconti. "I write a script, I give my installations a foreground, a background, a sequence shot . . . The people moving about in my interiors are my actors." She thinks of her residences as portraits. "I like people who have personal charm, who look better in the flesh than in photos. I try to reproduce that kind of grace in my decors."

Her interiors are striking for their natural quality, their user-friendly chic. She appreciates the simplicity of glazed clay, painted walls, rattan. And yet, as a glimpse of the panoply of materials (plush velvet, varieties of marble, fruit tree woods, leathers, gilded brass . . .) on hand in her studio reveals, she is constantly striving for sophistication. Mahdavi redraws the outlines of luxury. "I want to give my clients joy. People are much happier when they like their home." For each project, she immerses herself in the ambience of the place, its history, and of course the personalities of its occupants. She needs to maintain a dialogue with her clients, an exchange "like a photographer with a model." As she creates an interior, she uses her visual perception like a lens. "The blur of my nearsightedness is a very good tool for balancing volumes in space," she says. On the other hand, when she suspects a false note she takes a photo, which "instantly reveals what doesn't work in a decor."

After years of designing furniture for Christian Liaigre, she launched her studio in 1999, and by the early 2000s had already made herself known.

Her first notable commission was for the APT nightclub in New York, which she transformed into the posh loft of an imaginary French dandy. She even gave him a name: Bernard. Then she decorated the Townhouse Hotel in South Beach, the Miami area's first boutique hotel, with its rooftop terrace sprinkled with red waterbeds.

Her talent as a colorist stems from her American childhood. Born to an Iranian academic father and an Egyptian-British mother, Mahdavi spent her early years in Cambridge, Massachusetts, before a move to Germany that

India Mahdavi Dreaming in Color

she experienced as a chromatic shock, a sudden scene change "from a world in Technicolor to a world in black and white." She still takes pleasure in recalling images from the 1960s: "The cheerful colors of the 'Peanuts' comic strips, the lacquered lunchboxes, the candy-colored cars . . ." All of these childhood impressions influence the look of her interiors and her furniture designs. The latter always exude a fun, appetizing quality, like her already classic *Bishop* stool in enameled ceramic (2008) or her *Charlotte* armchair (2016), a puffy pink cake of a seat. Reliving visual memories, India Mahdavi has become a master of the flashback.

Axelle Corty

India Mahdavi in her showroom on rue Las Cases in Paris, a sumptuous showcase for her latest creations.

For *AD Intérieurs* 2011, India Mahdavi created a bedroom inspired by the paintings of Mark Rothko. The zoological motifs of the floor and fabrics stand out against the solid fields of color on the walls, creating an upbeat interplay of shapes and colors. The bed is by Maria Pergay. | FOLLOWING PAGES The living room of an old farmhouse in Connecticut, divided into two spaces: one near the window with two *Jelly Pea* sofas, and the other, more spacious, with *Bluffer* sofas. The coffee tables, console, and screens were designed by India Mahdavi. In between, the metal chairs by Jean Royère and the floor lamp, in the back to the right, date from the 1950s. In front of the fireplace are two André Arbus leather chairs and, on the left, a floor lamp by Andrea Branzi.

OPPOSITE AND ABOVE In a loft in eastern Paris, the small green-walled sitting room is furnished with a large marble and rosewood coffee table by Sergio Rodrigues, plus Mahdavi's *Œdipe* sofa and *Bishop* stool. The three *Téhéran* vases were created by Mahdavi for Bernardaud. The kitchen opens onto a living room conceived like a reception space. Woven synthetic fabric chairs by Franz West are arranged around a large oak and ceramic *Diagonale* table, designed by India Mahdavi. Colorful bowls and cups, produced for Mahdavi by Atelier Buffile, brighten the marble shelves. | FOLLOWING PAGES *Banana Leaves* wallpaper by Turnell & Gigon provides the backdrop for India Mahdavi's "Tropical Winter Garden" for *AD Intérieurs* 2010. The rattan bar, armchairs, and coffee tables are all Mahdavi's own designs.

The master bedroom of a Connecticut farmhouse features an India Mahdavi "total look," with her *Nouvelle Vague* sofas, bed, and rug, a monochromatic painting by the Canadian artist Agnes Martin, and, on the left, an *Amande* floor lamp by Christian Liaigre. On the nightstand is a vintage black ceramic lamp.

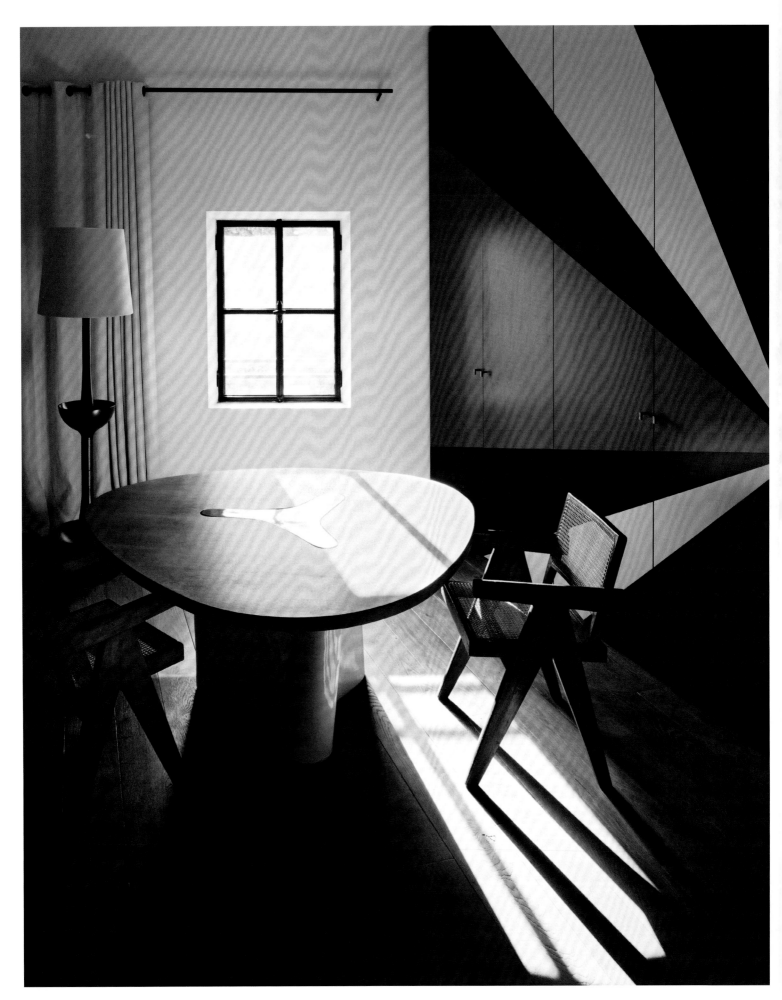

ABOVE A villa in Arles with a graphic decor. In one of the bedrooms, a large dressing room is hidden behind "radiating" Formica doors. The chairs around the walnut and ceramic *Diagonale* table are by Pierre Jeanneret. | OPPOSITE The bathroom is a vibrant composition combining psychedelic wallpaper, small *zellig* tiles, and an elaborately veined marble floor. The enameled ceramic *Bishop* stool and *Condesa* sink are Mahdavi designs.

On the upper level of a villa in Arles, a former bedroom has been converted into an office featuring a Pierre Jeanneret table, chairs by Jean Royère, and two *Siamese* sofas. In the background is a *Totem* shelf unit by Martino Gamper dating from 2007. The artwork on the wall is *Avengers Target* by Bozidar Brazda, 2006.

OPPOSITE This guest room at the Hôtel du Cloître in Arles sets up a lighthearted banter between the spiral headboard, the checked cashmere bedspread, the caned cabinet, the oak and metal nightstand, and a tile fragment floor with glass mosaic insets, all designed by India Mahdavi. The bedside lamp is by Serge Mouille. | ABOVE The north lobby is enhanced with an artwork by Matthew Brannon entitled *Gentleman's Relish*, a bookshelf holding colorful bottles. The *Bêta* lamp is by Mahdavi and the table and bench by Valentin Loellmann.

Isabelle Stanislas attributes her vocation to a nomadic childhood—her family moved a lot. From country to country, from one home to the next, she began to take an interest in decoration. After graduating from secondary school, she studied interior design before enrolling in the public architecture program at ENSBA (École Nationale Supérieure des Beaux Arts), the prestigious Paris art academy. "I understood that the architecture must create the context for the decor, and not the other way around," she explains. "For me, interior design is a matter of culture, taste, soul, and heart . . ."

Her education gave her a firm grasp of the concepts of light, volumes, traffic, and circulation patterns. "Architecture taught me everything about the key factors that I deal with today," she says. Those years also brought her first professional experiences. She formed a collective with a group of friends from ENSBA (architects, photographers, and landscape, graphic, and interior designers) and rented a workspace. "We submitted a lot of proposals in various fields," she recounts, "from music to video games, design, architecture . . ." She created her first decor while still a student, for an apartment whose appearance in the press brought her a second commission, for a townhouse. Until graduation she completed one project every year, combining architecture and interior design—the hybrid approach that she has cultivated ever since.

Armed with a degree in architecture, she then turned to the fast-paced world of fashion. Her first meeting with Thierry Gillier (the founder and owner of Zadig & Voltaire) marked a turning point: their collaboration lasted for twelve years, during which she developed the architectural concept of

his shops. Today she is much in demand among the luxury houses (Hermès, Cartier, Céline), designing furniture, working on special events, etc. And in parallel she continues to create spaces: old apartments that she converts and restores, lofts for which she pursues her reflection on the use of concrete (one of her favorite materials), vacation homes . . .

Stanislas's style is unmistakable: precision, a focus on the preparatory drawings, pure lines, and simplicity tempered by a desire for warmth, and a

Isabelle Stanislas
Graphic Constructs

rendering that she sees as arising from a "perfect balance of masculine and feminine." These are the qualities that also characterize the furniture and lighting systems that she designs, rethinking the function, pushing the limits of the materials, and taking pleasure in the research process. With projects all over Europe and beyond—from Paris to New York or Tel Aviv, from Ibiza to Comporta, Portugal—she handles everything from interior design to furniture creation and the construction of houses. A professional dream come true for this devoted, enthusiastic architect.

Françoise-Claire Prodhon

Isabelle Stanislas in the space that she created for the 2014 AD Intérieurs exhibition at the Musée des Arts Décoratifs.

Isabelle Stanislas updated this classic Parisian apartment with a mezzanine and a metal staircase, making use of the room's ample volumes. Her exacting composition integrates the original mirror and moldings as elements of contrast.

OPPOSITE AND ABOVE The living room–dining room conceived for the *AD Intérieurs* exhibition of 2015. The use of raw concrete lends sophistication to the illuminated metal structures, mirrored panels, and cactus garden. Above the lounge area is a neon work by the artist Daniel Firman.

soleil double

PREVIOUS PAGES The living room of the Soleil Suite at Domaine des Étangs, a castle converted into a luxury hotel in southwestern France. Balancing each other on either side of the window are a geometric wall lamp by Michael Anastassiades and the golden disk of *Soleil Double*, an artwork by Laurent Grasso. | ABOVE A Paris apartment with all-white walls and ceilings. In the entryway, a piece of driftwood from Bali is placed under a lamp by Serge Mouille. | OPPOSITE The lounge area of the Vénus Suite at Domaine des Étangs, an opulent boudoir-like space with a Louis XV chest of drawers, a nineteenth-century shell-shaped stool, and a perforated zinc lighting column by Fabio Cappello.

Under the nineteenth-century gilded coffered ceiling of the Paris home of Thierry Gillier, founder of the ready-to-wear label Zadig & Voltaire, Isabelle Stanislas set out to capture a loft-like spirit with exposed brick, stainless steel, and a dining room–kitchen open to the living room. The lamps in the kitchen and on the right are by the Bouroullec brothers and the large painting on the right is by Rudolf Stingel.

ABOVE In Paris, a white marble bathroom with a window overlooking the statues adorning the Louvre. | OPPOSITE *The Thinker*, a canvas by Jean-Michel Basquiat, is among the contemporary art in a bedroom of Thierry Gillier's residence in Paris.

PREVIOUS PAGES The entrance of Domaine des Étangs. The classic touches—Louis XVI consoles and ottoman, Louis XV mirrors—contrast with a contemporary chandelier designed by Isabelle Stanislas. | OPPOSITE Stanislas designed the straight-edged furniture for the "Homme" lounge at Domaine des Étangs, as well as the rug, an exclusive creation for the hotel. The artwork on the wall is *Image du Ciel Vu de Nuit. Stern 09h58 -40°* by Thomas Ruff. | ABOVE The library-bar composed for *AD Intérieurs* 2014 features two eye-catching materials: alabaster for the floor, bar, and sofa, and brass with a bronze finish.

Today he wonders if the impetus for his career choice came from a childhood experience in Marseille: the deep admiration that he harbored for his best friend's father. "He was an extremely talented man," Thierry Lemaire recalls, "who lived in a very contemporary apartment in a building from the 1970s, all white with artworks and touches of mahogany. Subconsciously, I recreated that same spirit in my own apartment." He also mentions that his mother had a natural flair for decoration, combining concrete with eighteenth-century furniture. After graduating from secondary school, he enrolled at the École Spéciale d'Architecture in Paris. In the late 1980s he launched his architectural firm, focusing at first on the construction of buildings. When business dropped off during the recession of the 1990s, he changed direction and began renovating apartments, thus entering what he calls "the world apart" of interior design.

The commissions kept coming, but, he says, his career really took off thanks to AD: "There was 'before AD' and 'after AD.'" His appearances in the magazine and decors created for the annual AD Intérieurs exhibition since 2010 have given him a high-profile showcase for his interiors and, above all, his furniture creations. In an attempt to define his style, it could be described as the juxtaposition of rough-hewn and precious materials, plus the dynamism of angular and contrasting or organic lines, all softened by curves inspired by the 1960s and '70s. To which one could add that this tall, handsome designer thinks big: he creates sofas measuring sixteen, twenty-three, or even thirty feet if the space calls for it. His interiors radiate a palpable energy, accentuated by a rather "brutalist" treatment of the materials that in no way detracts from the overall impression of refinement. Indeed,

he is accustomed to collaborating with top-level artisans like the straw marquetry specialist Lison de Caunes, the mosaicist Béatrice Serre, and Donato Coppola, an expert in resins and surface treatments. Lemaire creates interplays of metals, mirrored surfaces, and newly-developed finishes, the fruit of the latest research—like his flame-treated coffee table or his console with mixed resin panels seen at the AD exhibitions. It came as no surprise in 2014 when two furniture makers, Fendi in Italy and Holly Hunt in the United States, asked him to design collections for their catalogs. But as much as he loves developing his own pieces, he also enjoys scouring the antiques

Thierry Lemaire
A '70s Spirit

shops, from "Les Puces" in Paris to the Basel fair, seeking out collector's items for his clients. The Parisian antiques dealer Yves Gastou, who has commissioned Lemaire twice to create his stand for the Paris Biennale des Antiquaires, has the highest praise for the designer: "His eclectic visual sense gives him a unique capacity to assimilate pieces from the 1930s, '40s, '50s, '60s, and '70s, using them in elegant new combinations and contexts. He belongs to that rare breed of interior designers, like Henri Samuel, who know how to make vintage furniture the springboard for expressing exquisite taste." As for Lemaire himself, he strives above all to create spaces that will last over time, and that maintain a balance—even with "eccentric" furniture.

Aude de La Conté

Thierry Lemaire in the reflections on the windows of a duplex with a terrace in Beirut.

The living room of this seaside house in Comporta, Portugal, features coffee table–stools by Thierry Lemaire surrounded by a *Chromatique* sofa by Steiner.

OPPOSITE AND ABOVE The walls, floors, and ceilings of this Comporta house provide a dark background for colorful vintage pieces like the *DSW* chairs by Charles and Ray Eames. In the bedroom, Pierre Paulin's *577* chair dialogues with a photograph by the Portuguese artist Helena Almeida.

The Chinese-inspired lounge presented as part of *AD Intérieurs* 2012. The central element of the decor, a screen with mirrors and lacquered wood panels, was created by Thierry Lemaire, like the coffee table–stools in lacquered glass and brushed brass.

ABOVE AND OPPOSITE With his *Cabinet d'Esthète* ("Esthete's Study") created for the 2015 edition of *AD Intérieurs*, Thierry Lemaire presented his vision of jet-set brutalism, juxtaposing concrete with eighteenth-century woodwork and a black marble floor, hammered brass with brocade, a seventeenth-century Roman painting with a blackened steel table . . . The sofa, fireplace, table, coffee tables, and armchairs are all his own designs.

PREVIOUS PAGES For this chalet in Gstaad, Thierry Lemaire challenged tradition by creating an essentially wood-free decor. He designed the coffee table and the large two-tone sofa. The occasional tables are by Philippe Hiquily and the paintings above the fireplace by the American artist Teresita Fernández. | OPPOSITE AND ABOVE This Beirut apartment is bathed in shades of brown and beige from floor to ceiling. The dining room is separated from the living room by a stylized *mashrabiya*. The table and chairs are by Christian Liaigre and the photograph by Marc Quinn. The bedroom is decorated with Manila hemp. Lemaire designed the bed with its built-in table, lamps, and nightstand, and the photograph is by Simon Norfolk.

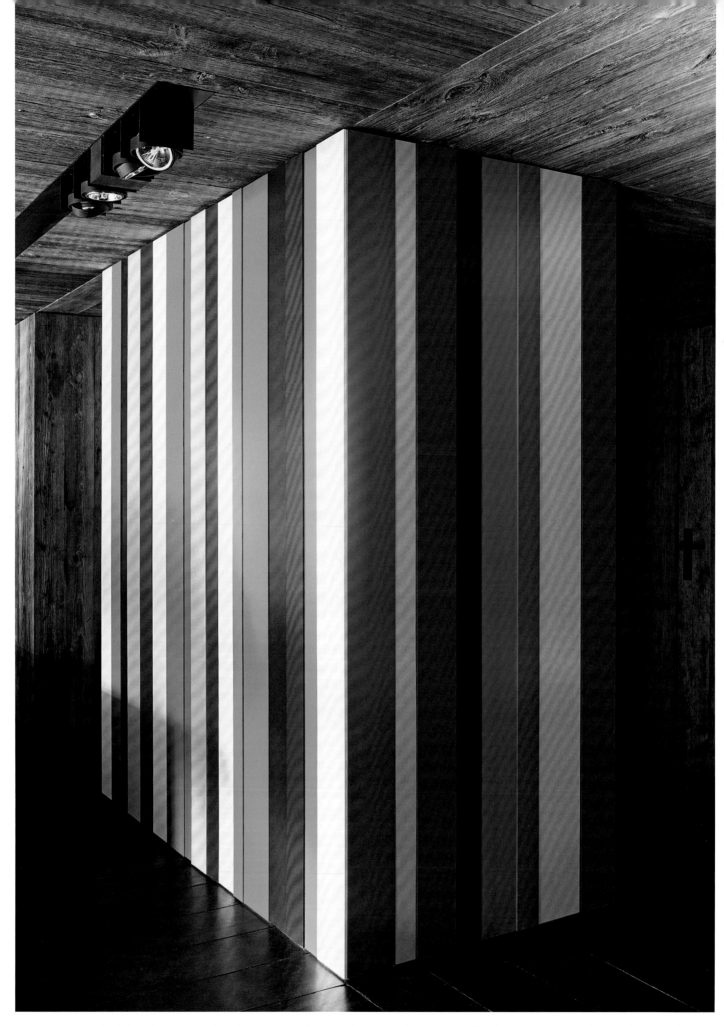

PREVIOUS PAGES A palette of grays for a chalet in Gstaad. The fireplace separates the living room from the dining room while remaining open on both sides. | ABOVE AND OPPOSITE For this new-look chalet in Gstaad, Thierry Lemaire started with planks of raw blackened wood. Standing out against this backdrop are a colorful striped dressing room in MDF, a steel bar by Gabriella Crespi from the 1960s, and a painting by the Portuguese artist José Pedro Croft.

The famous Paris café-bistro La Palette has been his unofficial headquarters for many years. He knows the neighborhood, between the Seine and the church of Saint-Germain-des-Prés, like the back of his hand. It was here, a stone's throw from his studio in a former art gallery on rue de Seine, that he completed his studies at the art school of the University of Paris 1. Having a gift for mathematics and a love of art, he gravitated toward architecture because, as he puts it, "It seemed to be the only path that combined the two things, math and art." Thus he found himself enrolled as an architecture student at a time when the coursework put the emphasis on technique, but without neglecting the humanities: he was much inspired and influenced by the thinking of the architecture and urban planning historian Jean-Louis Cohen.

The young Charles Zana supplemented this intellectual awakening with frequent visits to the nearby galleries, and found himself equally fascinated with the paintings, sculptures, and furniture on view in the antiques shops—especially the work of the big names from the 1930s, like Jean-Michel Frank, Pierre Chareau, and Robert Mallet-Stevens, who orchestrated the entire living space from the volumes to the door knobs and sofas. "It's part of the cultural wealth of Paris that we have such cultivated dealers who keep these treasures in circulation." He listened and learned—and experienced a new burst of enthusiasm in 1985 when a show devoted to Ettore Sottsass opened right outside his school at the gallery of Yves Gastou, who asked the Milanese avant-garde architect-designer to create his exhibition space. It was the beginning of Zana's passion for the Italians from Studio Alchimia and the Memphis Group: Andrea Branzi, Alessandro Mendini, Michele De Lucchi . . . Today he collects their ceramic and glass pieces, lending them for exhibitions in venues like the Musée Delacroix.

After graduating, Charles Zana headed for the United States in the late 1990s, where he learned to develop a global vision of each project. Returning to France, he began designing retail spaces for labels like Et Vous and Apostrophe, and soon branched out to private residences. In 2010 his reputation

Charles Zana
The Art of Allusion

got a boost from his participation in *AD Intérieurs*, his dining room for Caffè Artcurial, and an ever-increasing number of mentions in the press. His signature is readily identifiable: energetic lines, graphic compositions that avoid minimalism, fluid circulation, and an ongoing dialogue with artworks. His architectural background gives him an expert perception of space and light. "The French style is a classical style with a twist of modernity, of liberty," Zana comments. "The workmanship of France's artisans and specialist industries, highlighting materials like wood, marble, and metal, is a big part of the success of the 'French touch.' Today the great pastry chefs are reinventing classics like the Paris Brest—and we're doing the same thing with marble and molding. An architect's vision is an overall harmony, like the Maison de Verre in Paris or Villa Necchi in Milan. It's all about putting some feeling into the space."

Aude de La Conté

Charles Zana in one of his interiors. On the left is an artwork entitled *We The People* by Danh Vo, and on the right one of Zana's own creations, the *Nomad Stool*.

As its name implies, the *Salon de Bain* ("Bath–Living Room") for *AD Intérieurs* 2014 combines elements of a living room—a bookshelf, sofa, and armchairs by Charles Zana, a coffee table by Martin Szekely—with marble and brass washroom fixtures.

OPPOSITE For *AD Intérieurs* 2013, Charles Zana composed a sculptural living room–kitchen with a marble counter and a large bookcase-pantry backed with 1950s-style tiles. | ABOVE In a townhouse in the Paris suburbs, a banister edged with stainless steel and a "necklace" by the artist Jean-Michel Othoniel linking the two levels. | FOLLOWING PAGES The living room section of Zana's living room–kitchen for *AD Intérieurs* 2013. The rug and sofa were designed by Zana and the burnt wood coffee tables are by Normal Studio.

ABOVE In a lounge area of this Parisian art collector's house, an illuminated piece by Jenny Holzer is displayed alongside a Tom Wesselmann painting. In the foreground are an Italian sofa from the 1970s and a Pierre Charpin coffee table in brushed lacquered aluminum. | OPPOSITE In the house's spacious living room, a Ron Arad chair, placed on a leather rug by Agnès Comar, gleams with highlights in front of an artwork by Chun Kwang Young from his *Aggrégation* series and, in the background, *Assemblage 4* by the Bouroullec brothers.

This vast Paris apartment was conceived to house a contemporary art collection. Under its skylights, the living room becomes a gallery in which daily life shares the space with a hyperrealist sculpture by Duane Hanson and paintings by contemporary artists.

ABOVE AND OPPOSITE For this duplex in a Parisian townhouse, Charles Zana favored a pop-chic look with colorful kinetic art. The dining room has a nightclub-like feel, lit with glimmering *Sparkle Shady* lamps by Jaime Hayon. The living room pulses to the beat of an op art rug by Yaacov Agam, a Pierre Paulin sofa, two Pucci de Rossi coffee tables, and, in the background, from left to right, sculptures by Man Ray and Jean-Claude Farhi and a floor lamp by Philippe Hiquily.

In this Paris apartment with a terrace overlooking the Arc de Triomphe, orange seats by Giovanni Offredi encircle a Pierre Charpin coffee table. In the foreground is a cubic console by Ron Arad, who also created the lounge chair in front of the window. The sculpture is by Erwin Wurm and the pendant lamp by Jacopo Foggini.

OPPOSITE *The curve of the living room of this apartment in western Paris set the tone for the decor. The furnishings include a rounded sofa and a silk rug designed by Charles Zana, an armchair and* Liane *floor lamp by Jean Royère, and a Ron Arad table.* | ABOVE *In the same apartment, a dark two-tone bookcase provides an element of contrast. In the foreground is a saucer-like lamp by Yonel Lebovici. The* Model U *table is by Eric Schmitt and the* Aim *pendant lamp by the Bouroullec brothers.*

The Best
Address Book
In Paris

From designer furniture to art and antiques, Paris is home to a great many rare, unique shops and showrooms that play a key role in the ongoing vitality of French interior design. The number of galleries has grown rapidly in recent years, and since the turn of the century a new generation of experts like Emmanuel Perrotin has strengthened Paris's reputation as an international capital of contemporary art. In this decade, we have seen a rise in the number of spaces spotlighting limited-edition or one-of-a-kind furniture, exemplified by Carpenters Workshop Gallery. Whether due to a lack of period pieces or the prohibitive prices commanded by the famous names of the past, many specialists in twentieth-century antiques are also exhibiting contemporary talents. Most recently we have seen a proliferation of furniture lines using precious materials, produced in small series by interior designers. Some, like Bruno Moinard, have opened spaces dedicated to their refined creations.

Design Galleries

88 Gallery

Philippe Rapin divides his time between Paris and Hong Kong, and among three activities: designer, antiques dealer, and gallery owner, spotlighting furniture by Paolo Buffa, Piero Fornasetti, Gio Ponti, and Kam Tin, as well as mirrors, chandeliers, and jewelry by Robert Goossens.

25 quai Voltaire
75007 Paris
+ 33 (0)1 42 61 24 21
www.house-rapin.com

Galerie Avant-Scène

For the past thirty years, gallery director and decorator Elisabeth Delacarte has been spotlighting precious, poetic creations with a baroque flavor. With pieces by Franck Evennou, Hubert Le Gall, or Elisabeth Garouste, the Parisian spirit of Avant-Scène is a magnet for collectors.

4 place de l'Odeon
75006 Paris
+ 33 (0)1 46 33 12 40
www.avantscene.fr

Galerie BSL

Nacho Carbonell, Faye Toogood, Noé Duchaufour-Lawrance . . . The pieces featured by BSL are as eclectic as they are chic, spanning the range from the spectacular to the minimalist, from the artisanal to the technological.

23 rue Charlot
75003 Paris
+ 33 (0)1 44 78 94 14
www.galeriebsl.com

Carpenters Workshop Gallery

At the frontier between art and design, Carpenters Workshop produces limited editions of pieces by Studio Job, Atelier van Lieshout, Ingrid Donat, Rick Owens, etc., with spaces in London, Paris, and New York. In less than ten years, the gallery has become internationally known for its glamorous vision of design.

54 rue de la Verrerie
75004 Paris
+ 33 (0)1 42 78 80 92
www.carpentersworkshopgallery.com

Galerie Carole Decombe

From vintage Scandinavian pieces to contemporary design, Carole Decombe exhibits everything that catches her eye, in Paris and at her new branch gallery in Los Angeles.

30 rue de Lille
75007 Paris
+ 33 (0)1 40 20 00 12
www.galeriecaroledecombe.com

Galerie Gosserez

Just down the street from the Musée Picasso, this gallery offers limited editions by a handful of young talents from around the world, including the French designer Éric Jourdan.

3 rue Debelleyme
75003 Paris
+ 33 6 12 29 90 40
www.galeriegosserez.com

Galerie En Attendant les Barbares

Since 1983, En Attendant les Barbares has pursued the approach of producing refined furniture and decorative objects by now-historic names like Garouste & Bonetti, Olivier Gagnère, Andrée Putman, Eric Schmitt, Matt Sindall . . .

35 rue de Grenelle
75007 Paris
+ 33 (0)1 42 22 65 25
www.barbares.com

Galerie kreo

With spaces in Paris and London, the gallery founded by Clémence and Didier Krzentowski is a longtime favorite among design aficionados. A pioneer in its field, Galerie kreo functions as a creative laboratory, producing limited editions by the most prominent designers and offering selections of vintage lamps and furniture.

31 rue Dauphine
75006 Paris
+ 33 (0)1 53 10 23 00
www.galeriekreo.com

Galerie Mougin

Furniture, jewelry, and the decorative arts: in the heart of the Left Bank, Gladys Mougin explores the precious worlds of designers like Laurence Montano and André Dubreuil.

22 and 30 rue de Lille
75007 Paris
+ 33 (0)1 40 20 08 33
www.galeriemougin.com

Auction Houses

Galerie Armel Soyer

This young gallery specializes in the decorative arts of the twenty-first century, producing and promoting the creations of a new generation of artists and artisans.

19 rue Chapon
75003 Paris
+ 33 (0)1 42 55 49 72
www.armelsoyer.com

Tools Galerie

Loïc Bigot has moved from the Marais to the Left Bank, in the process broadening the scope of his offering. At Tools Galerie, design flirts with the baroque or conceptual art, and artisanal craftsmanship goes hand-in-hand with technology.

1 rue Montalembert
75007 Paris
+ 33 (0)1 84 05 96 64
www.toolsgalerie.com

Artcurial

Occupying a stately townhouse on the Champs-Élysées, France's leading auction house owes its reputation to the diversity of its offerings. A pioneer in auctions of collector's automobiles and comic books, Artcurial covers the entire cultural-artistic spectrum.

7 rond-point des Champs-Élysées
75008 Paris
+ 33 (0)1 42 99 20 20
www.artcurial.com

Christie's

Founded by James Christie in London in 1766, the world's biggest auction house has been owned since 1998 by the eminent art collector François Pinault. With operations around the globe, Christie's hosts auctions in more than eighty specialty fields.

9 avenue Matignon
75008 Paris
+ 33 (0)1 40 76 85 85
www.christies.com

Drouot

Paris's largest auction house is named after the Right Bank street that has been its home since the 1850s. With its twenty auction rooms, Drouot is a veritable museum, popular with treasure hunters, antiques dealers, and tourists.

9 rue Drouot
75009 Paris
+ 33 (0)1 48 00 20 20
www.drouot.com

Piasa

Founded in 1996 and located in Paris's "Golden Triangle" since 2014, Piasa has made twentieth-century design one of its specialties, with a focus on creations from Scandinavia, Italy, etc. The house also holds two auctions a year devoted to interior designers, organized in partnership with *AD* France.

118 rue du Faubourg Saint-Honoré
75008 Paris
+ 33 (0)1 53 34 10 10
www.piasa.fr

Sotheby's

Founded in London in 1744 and now active in forty countries and seventy specialty fields, Sotheby's is one of the top international auction houses. At Galerie Charpentier, across the street from the presidential palace, it hosts some thirty auctions in Paris every year.

76 rue du Faubourg Saint-Honoré
75008 Paris
+ 33 (0)1 53 05 53 05
www.sothebys.com

Twentieth-Century Antiques

Galerie L'Arc en Seine

For more than thirty years, this Parisian gallery has been a mainstay for art deco collectors, presenting pieces by Pierre Chareau, Paul Dupre-Lafon, Jean-Michel Frank . . .

31 rue de Seine
75006 Paris
+ 33 (0)1 43 29 11 02
www.arcenseine.com

Galerie Alexandre Biaggi

A specialist in the decorative arts of the 1920s through the '50s, Alexandre Biaggi also offers his advice as a decorator, along with a sophisticated selection of antiques and contemporary pieces.

14 rue de Seine
75006 Paris
+ 33 (0)1 44 07 34 73
www.alexandrebiaggi.com

Galerie Jean-Louis Danant

At this gallery, diversity is the rule. Jean-Louis Danant chooses furniture, decorative objects, and artworks produced between 1930 and 1980, creating an intriguing visual interaction among the pieces on display.

36 avenue Matignon
75008 Paris
+ 33 (0)1 42 89 40 15
www.galerie-danant.com

Galerie Downtown
François Laffanour

From the Steph Simon years to the creations of Takis, Pucci de Rossi, and Ron Arad, François Laffanour has chosen some of the most illustrious signatures from the history of architecture, art, and design.

18 rue de Seine
75006 Paris
+ 33 (0)1 46 33 82 14
www.galeriedowntown.com

Galerie Anne-Sophie Duval

Championing the rediscovery of art deco for more than forty years, this gallery features works by the most remarkable designers of the early twentieth century.

50 quai Malaquais
75006 Paris
+ 33 (0)1 43 54 51 16
www.annesophieduval.com

Galerie Patrick Fourtin

A bit off the beaten track, Patrick Fourtin's space blends art and design from the 1930s through the '90s with works by the designers of today.

9 rue des Bons Enfants
75001 Paris
+ 33 (0)1 42 60 12 63
www.galeriefourtin.com

Galerie Yves Gastou

In the 1980s Yves Gastou introduced Memphis and Italian design to Paris. Today, with the help of his son, he continues to break new ground, often with surprisingly original creations.

12 rue Bonaparte
75006 Paris
+ 33 (0)1 53 73 00 10
www.galerieyvesgastou.com

Galerie Oscar Graf

This gallery shows pieces from the era that laid the groundwork for modernism, from 1870 to 1910. An astute choice that immediately placed Oscar Graf among Paris's most prominent antique dealers.

15 rue de Seine
75006 Paris
+ 33 (0)1 82 09 14 84
www.oscar-graf.com

Galerie James

Since 2011, Paul and Candice Viguier have been introducing Parisians to the most beautiful examples of Brazilian modernist design from the 1950s and '60s.

20 rue de Thorigny
75003 Paris
+ 33 (0)1 40 09 97 41
www.james-paris.com

Jousse Entreprise

Philippe Jousse's Left Bank gallery specializes in furniture by architects and the creations of Jean Prouvé, Charlotte Perriand, Mathieu Matégot, Serge Mouille, Roger Tallon, Michel Boyer, etc. He also has a space in the Marais devoted to contemporary art.

18 rue de Seine
75006 Paris
+ 33 (0)1 53 82 13 60
www.jousse-company.com

Galerie Jacques Lacoste
From Jean Royère to Max Ingrand and Alexandre Noll, this art historian turned antiques dealer explores the decorative arts of the twentieth century, uncovering its most precious treasures.
12 rue de Seine
75006 Paris
+ 33 (0)1 40 20 41 82
www.jacqueslacoste.com

Galerie Marcilhac
As director of the gallery founded by his father in 1969, Félix Marcilhac seeks out the best of the twentieth-century decorative arts.
8 rue Bonaparte
75006 Paris
+ 33 (0)1 43 26 47 36
www.marcilhacgalerie.com

Galerie du Passage
Inspired and adventuresome, on a perpetual quest for beautiful objects in the spirit of Madeleine Castaing (perhaps his role model . . .), Pierre Passebon has built a reputation for his eclectic offerings. His customers come seeking the exceptional.
20-26 passage Véro-Dodat
75001 Paris
+ 33 (0)1 42 36 01 13
www.galeriedupassage.com

Galerie Eric Philippe
Since opening his gallery in 1980, Eric Philippe has offered an enlightened perspective on the history of the European and American decorative arts in the twentieth century, exhibiting pieces by big names like Jean-Michel Frank, Paavo Tynell, Frank Lloyd Wright, and Alvar Aalto.
25 passage Véro-Dodat
75001 Paris
+ 33 (0)1 42 33 28 26
www.ericphilippe.com

Les Puces de Saint-Ouen flea market–Paul-Bert/Serpette
With no fewer than 350 stands, Paul Bert/Serpette is the world's largest antiques market. Spanning the spectrum from ancient Egypt to the twentieth century, from curios to masterpieces, this landmark draws crowds of casual browsers and professionals alike.
96-110 rue des Rosiers
18 rue Paul Bert
93400 Saint Ouen
+ 33 (0)1 40 11 54 14
www.paulbertserpette.com

Galerie Chastel Maréchal
From Serge Roche to Yonel Lebovici, some of the most outstanding examples of the French decorative arts from the 1930s through the '70s are on view at Aline Chastel's gallery.
5 rue Bonaparte
75006 Paris
+ 33 (0)1 40 46 82 61
www.chastel-marechal.com

Galerie Vallois
Devotees of art deco (Jean Besnard, Armand-Albert Rateau, Émile-Jacques Ruhlmann . . .), Cheska and Bob Vallois have been promoting its rediscovery for more than forty years.
41 rue de Seine
75006 Paris
+ 33 (0)1 43 29 50 84
www.vallois.com

Galerie Patrick Seguin
Patrick Seguin has galleries in Paris and London showing pieces by the biggest names in modernist design, from Jean Prouvé to Charlotte Perriand, Le Corbusier, Pierre Jeanneret, and Jean Royère.
5 rue des Taillandiers
75011 Paris
+ 33 (0)1 47 00 32 35
www.patrickseguin.com

Interior Design Galleries

Galerie Cat Berro

Tradition meets modernity: since 2006 Cat Berro has produced and exhibited one-of-a-kind and limited-edition pieces by the biggest names in design, from Mattia Bonetti to Olivier Gagnère, Pucci de Rossi and Eric Schmitt.

25 rue Guénégaud
75006 Paris
+ 33 (0)1 43 25 58 10
www.catberro.fr

Chahan Gallery

Offering antiques, period furniture, and contemporary creations (including his own), Chahan Minassian cultivates a chic, sophisticated style that has won him an international clientele.

11 rue de Lille
75007 Paris
+ 33 (0)1 47 03 47 00
www.chahan.com

Christophe Delcourt
Maison d'Édition

Favoring raw textures and elegant lines, this ardent champion of French artisanal traditions launched his furniture company in the late 1990s. Since then his catalog has been enriched with his own creations as well as exclusive editions by guest designers like Laurent Nicolas and Tristan Auer.

47 rue de Babylone
75007 Paris
+ 33 (0)1 42 71 34 84
www.christophedelcourt.com

Liaigre

A pared-down style, a devotion to fine materials, and artisanal production . . . For the past thirty years, designer Christian Liaigre has been reinventing contemporary classicism with understated elegance.

42 rue du Bac
75007 Paris
+ 33 (0)1 53 63 33 66
www.christian.liaigre.fr

India Mahdavi

Since founding her firm in 2000, this architect-designer has developed a distinctive signature, playing up contrasts and controlled dissonance in an updated '70s spirit. Characterized by a daring use of color, her creations are instantly appealing.

3 rue Las Cases
75007 Paris
+ 33 (0)1 45 55 67 67
www.india-mahdavi.com

Galerie May

From marquetry to lacquerware and ceramics, the architect-interior designer Charles Tassin fills his gallery with furniture and objects in the finest artisanal tradition.

23 rue de Lille
75007 Paris
+ 33 (0)1 42 61 41 40
www.galerie-may.fr

Galerie Bruno Moinard Éditions

With pure lines, sumptuous materials, and soigné finishing, the creations by Bruno Moinard express an architect's vision of design, a tasteful interpretation of timeless classicism.

31 rue Jacob
75006 Paris
+ 33 (0)1 77 15 67 06
www.brunomoinardeditions.com

Pinto Paris

A vision of interior design that embraces all styles from the most classical to the contemporary, united by a dedication to impeccable craftsmanship. The spirit of Alberto and Linda Pinto is embodied in refined creations including furniture, accessories, and tableware.

14 rue du Mail
75002 Paris
+ 33 (0)1 40 13 00 00
www.pintoparis.com

Galerie Hervé Van der Straeten

Furniture, lamps, mirrors, jewelry . . . For three decades, Hervé Van der Straeten has based his eclectic style on a subtle balance between sculptural sensibility and functionality. Upholding the tradition of the French decorative arts, his creations have earned him a place among the Entreprises du Patrimoine Vivant (Living Heritage Companies) since 2007.

11 rue Ferdinand Duval
75004 Paris
+ 33 (0)1 42 78 99 99
www.vanderstraeten.fr

Galerie Tino Zervudachi

At Palais Royal, Tino Zervudachi spotlights the mixture of genres and periods that has made his reputation. His gallery is known as a source of exceptional furniture, objects, and artworks.

54 galerie Montpensier
jardin du Palais-Royal
75001 Paris
+ 33 (0)1 42 96 08 62
www.galerietz.com

Contemporary Art Galleries

Galerie Chantal Crousel

Over the past forty years, Chantal Crousel, now assisted by her son Niklas Svennung, has acquired a reputation for exacting choices and incisive programming, establishing long-term collaborations with an international roster of artists: Mona Hatoum, Thomas Hirschhorn, Jean-Luc Moulène, Anri Sala . . .

10 rue Charlot
75003 Paris
+ 33 (0)1 42 77 38 87
www.crousel.com

Galerie Kamel Mennour

With two addresses on the Left Bank and a third not far from the Champs-Élysées, Kamel Mennour is a pillar of the Paris art scene.

47 rue Saint-André-des-Arts
75006 Paris
+ 33 (0)1 56 24 03 63
www.kamelmennour.com

Galerie Perrotin

Long considered Paris's young lion of contemporary art, he helped launch Maurizio Cattelan, Takashi Murakami, and JR. With spaces in Paris, New York, Hong Kong, and Seoul, Emmanuel Perrotin continues to build on an already stellar reputation.

76 rue de Turenne
75003 Paris
+ 33 (0)1 42 16 79 79
www.perrotin.com

Almine Rech Gallery

James Turrell, Jeff Koons, and Richard Prince, as well as Bertrand Lavier, Tursic & Mille, and Taryn Simon: Almine Rech alternates between stars of the art market and young talents at her three galleries in Paris, Brussels, and London.

64 rue de Turenne
75003 Paris
+ 33 (0)1 45 83 71 90
www.alminerech.com

Galerie Thaddaeus Ropac

Since 1983, in Salzburg, Paris, and Pantin, soon to be joined by London, this elegant Austrian-born art dealer has been developing a prestigious international offering, including names like Georg Baselitz, Anselm Kiefer, Alex Katz, Gilbert & George, Tony Cragg, and Robert Longo.

7 rue Debelleyme
75003 Paris
+ 33 (0)1 42 72 99 00
www.ropac.net

Tornabuoni Art

This gallery specializes in Italian art from the second half of the twentieth century: Fontana, Manzoni, and Boetti, plus forerunners like Balla and De Chirico. Founded in Florence by Roberto Casamonti, Tornabuoni has been active in Paris since 2009, and also has spaces in Milan and London.

16 avenue Matignon
75008 Paris
+ 33 (0)1 53 53 51 51
www.tornabuoniart.fr

Photography Credits

p. 11
Photo Yannick Labrousse,
production Cédric Saint André Perrin

pp. 12-13
Photo Adrien Dirand
© 2016 Artists Rights Society (ARS),
New York / ADAGP, Paris

pp. 14-15
Photos Adrien Dirand

pp. 16-17
Photo Adrien Dirand
© 2016 Artists Rights Society (ARS),
New York / ADAGP, Paris
© The Estate of Jean-Michel Basquiat
/ ADAGP, Paris / ARS, New York 2016

pp. 18-19
Photos Adrien Dirand,
production Olivier Foltzer
© 2016 Artists Rights Society (ARS),
New York / ADAGP, Paris
© 2016 Artists Rights Society (ARS),
New York / AUTVIS, São Paulo

pp. 20-21
Photo Adrien Dirand,
production Olivier Foltzer

pp. 22-23
Photos Adrien Dirand
© 2016 Artists Rights Society (ARS),
New York / ADAGP, Paris
© 2016 Artists Rights Society (ARS),
New York / AUTVIS, São Paulo
© F.L.C. / ADAGP, Paris / Artists Rights
Society (ARS), New York 2016

pp. 24-25
Photo Yannick Labrousse,
production Cédric Saint André Perrin

p. 26
Photo Adrien Dirand,
production Olivier Foltzer
© 2016 Artists Rights Society (ARS),
New York / ADAGP, Paris

p. 27
Photo Adrien Dirand,
production Marie Kalt
© 2016 Artists Rights Society (ARS),
New York / ADAGP, Paris

p. 28
Photo Jason Schmidt,
production Sophie Pinet

pp. 30-31
Photo Jason Schmidt,
production Sophie Pinet

pp. 32-33
Photos Gonzalo Machado,
production Cédric Saint André Perrin

pp. 34-35
Photos Gonzalo Machado,
production Cédric Saint André Perrin

pp. 36-37
Photos Alexis Armanet,
production Sophie Pinet

p. 38
Photo Jason Schmidt,
production Sophie Pinet

p. 39
Photo Alexis Armanet,
production Sophie Pinet

pp. 40-41
Photo Yannick Labrousse,
production Cédric Saint André Perrin

p. 42
Photo Jérôme Galland,
production Thibaut Mathieu

p. 43
Photo Claire Israël,
production Cédric Saint André Perrin

pp. 44-45
Photos Jason Schmidt,
production Sophie Pinet

p. 46
Photo Yannick Labrousse,
production Cédric Saint André Perrin

pp. 48-49
Photo Jérôme Galland,
production Sylvie Thébaud

pp. 50-51
Photos Jason Schmidt,
production Mallery Roberts Morgan

pp. 52-53
Photos Jérôme Galland,
production Sylvie Thébaud
© 2016 Artists Rights Society (ARS),
New York / ADAGP, Paris

pp. 54-55
Photo Claire Israël,
production Cédric Saint André Perrin

pp. 56-57
Photos Magnus Marding,
production Olivier Foltzer
© 2016 Artists Rights Society (ARS),
New York / ADAGP, Paris

pp. 58-59
Photos Jérôme Galland,
production Sylvie Thébaud

pp. 60-61
Photo Julien Oppenheim,
production Cédric Saint André Perrin

pp. 62-63
Photos Philippe Garcia,
production Marie Kalt

p. 64
Photo Yannick Labrousse,
production Cédric Saint André Perrin

pp. 66-67
Photo Jérôme Galland,
production Françoise Claire Prodhon
© 2016 Artists Rights Society (ARS),
New York / VG Bild-Kunst, Bonn

p. 68
Photo Jérôme Galland,
production Françoise Claire Prodhon

p. 69
Photo Matthieu Salvaing,
production Marie Kalt

pp. 70-71
Photos Yannick Labrousse,
production Cédric Saint André Perrin

pp. 72-73
Photo Matthieu Salvaing,
production Marie Kalt
© 2016 Artists Rights Society (ARS),
New York / ADAGP, Paris
© 2016 Estate of Harry Bertoia / Artists
Rights Society (ARS), New York

p. 74
Photo Yannick Labrousse,
production Cédric Saint André Perrin

p. 75
Photo Jérôme Galland,
production Françoise Claire Prodhon

pp. 76-77
Photo Jérôme Galland,
production Olivier Foltzer

p. 78
Photo Yannick Labrousse,
production Cédric Saint André Perrin

p. 79
Photo Yannick Labrousse,
production Cédric Saint André Perrin

p. 80
Photo Jérôme Galland,
production Olivier Foltzer

p. 81
Photo Matthieu Salvaing,
production Marie Kalt

p. 82
Photo Matthieu Salvaing,
production Ana Cardinale

pp. 84-85
Photo Matthieu Salvaing,
production Ana Cardinale

p. 86
Photo Matthieu Salvaing,
production Ana Cardinale

p. 87
Photo Gonzalo Machado,
production Cédric Saint André Perrin

pp. 88-89
Photos Michael Paul/Living Inside

pp. 90-91
Photo Jérôme Galland,
production Esther Henwood

p. 92
Photo Jérôme Galland,
production Esther Henwood
© 2016 Artists Rights Society (ARS),
New York / ADAGP, Paris

p. 93
Photo Michael Paul/Living Inside

p. 94
Photo Sisters Agency
© 2016 Artists Rights Society (ARS),
New York / ADAGP, Paris

p. 95
Photo Jérôme Galland,
production Esther Henwood

pp. 96-97
Photos Michael Paul/Living Inside

p. 98
Photo Jérôme Galland,
production Esther Henwood
© 2016 Artists Rights Society (ARS),
New York / ADAGP, Paris

p. 99
Photo Mathieu Salvaing

p. 100
Photo Jérôme Galland,
production Marie Kalt
© 2016 Estate of Harry Bertoia / Artists
Rights Society (ARS), New York
© 2016 Artists Rights Society (ARS),
New York / ADAGP, Paris

pp. 102-103
Photo Claire Israël,
production Cédric Saint André Perrin
© 2016 Estate of Harry Bertoia / Artists
Rights Society (ARS), New York

pp. 104-105
Photos Jérôme Galland,
production Marie Kalt

pp. 106-107
Photo Gonzalo Machado,
production Olivier Foltzer

pp. 108-109
Photos Jérôme Galland,
production Marie Kalt

pp. 110-111
Photo Yannick Labrousse,
production Cédric Saint André Perrin
© 2016 Artists Rights Society (ARS),
New York / ADAGP, Paris

pp. 112-113
Photos Yannick Labrousse,
production Cédric Saint André Perrin
© 2016 Artists Rights Society (ARS),
New York / ADAGP, Paris

pp. 114-115
Photo Jérôme Galland,
production Marie Kalt
© 2016 Richard Serra / Artists Rights
Society (ARS), New York

pp. 116-117
Photos Jérôme Galland,
production Marie Kalt
© 2016 Artists Rights Society (ARS),
New York / ADAGP, Paris

p. 118
Photo Yannick Labrousse,
production Cédric Saint André Perrin
© 2016 Artists Rights Society (ARS),
New York / VG Bild-Kunst, Bonn

pp. 120-121
Photo Vincent Leroux,
production Esther Henwood

pp. 122-123
Photos Vincent Leroux,
production Esther Henwood
© 2016 Artists Rights Society (ARS),
New York / ADAGP, Paris

p. 124
Photo Vincent Leroux,
production Esther Henwood

p. 125
Photo Yannick Labrousse,
production Cédric Saint André Perrin

pp. 126-127
Photo Philippe Garcia,
production Olivier Foltzer

pp. 128-129
Photos Paul Lepreux,
production Olivier Foltzer

pp. 130-131
Photos Julien Oppenheim,
production Thibaut Mathieu

pp. 132-133
Photo Julien Oppenheim,
production Thibaut Mathieu

pp. 134-135
Photos Philippe Garcia,
production Olivier Foltzer
© 2016 Artists Rights Society (ARS),
New York / VG Bild-Kunst, Bonn

p. 136
Photo Gonzalo Machado,
production Cédric Saint André Perrin

pp. 138-139
Photo Olivier Amsellem,
production Olivier Foltzer
© 2016 Artists Rights Society (ARS),
New York / ADAGP, Paris

pp. 140-141
Photos Guillaume Grasset

p. 142
Photo Yannick Labrousse,
production Cédric Saint André Perrin

p. 143
Photo Gonzalo Machado,
production Cédric Saint André Perrin

pp. 144-145
Photo Olivier Amsellem

p. 146
Photo Frédéric de Gasquet

p. 147
Photo Olivier Amsellem

pp. 148-149
Photos Yannick Labrousse,
production Cédric Saint André Perrin

pp. 150-151
Photos Philippe Garcia,
production Cédric Saint André Perrin

pp. 152-153
Photos Olivier Amsellem,
production Olivier Foltzer

p. 154
Photo Claire Israël

pp. 156-157
Photo Jean-François Jaussaud /
Luxproductions
© 2016 Artists Rights Society (ARS),
New York / ADAGP, Paris

pp. 158-159
Photo Jason Schmidt
production Sarah Medford,
styling Michael Reynolds,
AD U.S. October 2014
© 2016 Artists Rights Society (ARS),
New York / ADAGP, Paris

pp. 160-161
Photos Matthieu Salvaing

pp. 162-163
Photo Jean-François Jaussaud /
Luxproductions

pp. 164-165
Photo Jason Schmidt
production Sarah Medford,
styling Michael Reynolds,
AD U.S. October 2014
© 2016 Agnes Martin / Artists Rights
Society (ARS), New York

pp. 166-167
Photos Philippe Garcia,
production Olivier Foltzer
© 2016 Artists Rights Society (ARS),
New York / ADAGP, Paris

pp. 168-169
Photos Philippe Garcia,
production Olivier Foltzer
© 2016 Artists Rights Society (ARS),
New York / ADAGP, Paris

p. 170
Photo Matthieu Salvaing

p. 171
François Halard

p. 172
Photo Gonzalo Machado,
production Cédric Saint André Perrin

pp. 174-175
Photo Olivier Loser

pp. 176-177
Photos Gonzalo Machado,
production Cédric Saint André Perrin

pp. 178-179
Photo Olivier Loser

p. 180
Photo Vincent Leroux,
production Olivier Foltzer

p. 181
Photo Olivier Loser

pp. 182-183
Photo Alexis Armanet,
production Olivier Foltzer

p. 184
Photo Vincent Leroux,
production Olivier Foltzer

p. 185
Photo Alexis Armanet,
production Olivier Foltzer
© The Estate of Jean-Michel Basquiat
/ ADAGP, Paris / ARS, New York 2016

pp. 186-187
Photo Olivier Loser

p. 188
Photo Gonzalo Machado,
production Cédric Saint André Perrin
© 2016 Artists Rights Society (ARS),
New York / VG Bild-Kunst, Bonn

p. 189
Photo Olivier Loser

p. 190
Photo Alexis Armanet,
production Marie Kalt

pp. 192-193
Photo Julien Oppenheim,
production Sylvie Thébaud

pp. 194-195
Photos Julien Oppenheim,
production Sylvie Thébaud

pp. 196-197
Photo Yannick Labrousse,
production Cédric Saint André Perrin

pp. 198-199
Photos Gonzalo Machado,
production Cédric Saint André Perrin

pp. 200-201
Photo Reto Guntli
© 2016 Artists Rights Society (ARS),
New York / ADAGP, Paris

pp. 202-203
Photos Alexis Armanet,
production Marie Kalt

pp. 204-205
Photo Adrien Dirand,
production Sylvie Thébaud

pp. 206-207
Photos Adrien Dirand,
production Sylvie Thébaud

p. 208
Photo Yannick Labrousse

pp. 210-211
Photo Claire Israël,
production Cédric Saint André Perrin

p. 212
Photo Claire Israël,
production Cédric Saint André Perrin

p. 213
Photo Jacques Pépion
© 2016 Artists Rights Society (ARS),
New York / ADAGP, Paris

pp. 214-215
Photo Claire Israël,
production Cédric Saint André Perrin

pp. 216-217
Photos Philippe Garcia

pp. 218-219
Photo Philippe Garcia

pp. 220-221
Photos Mai-Linh,
production Cédric Saint André Perrin
© 2016 Artists Rights Society (ARS),
New York / ADAGP, Paris
© Man Ray Trust / Artists Rights Society
(ARS), NY / ADAGP, Paris 2016

pp. 222-223
Photo Mai-Linh,
production Olivier Foltzer
© 2016 Artists Rights Society (ARS),
New York / Bildrecht, Vienna

pp. 224-225
Photos Jacques Pépion

Cover
Photo Vincent Leroux,
production Esther Henwood

Acknowledgments

Marie Kalt would like to thank the interior designers Tristan Auer, Buttazzoni & Associés, Vincent Darré, Jean-Louis Deniot, Joseph Dirand, Gilles & Boissier, Thierry Lemaire, India Mahdavi, Chahan Minassian, Isabelle Stanislas, Pierre Yovanovitch, and Charles Zana for their participation in the preparation of this book as well as their unwavering support for *AD* magazine (*Architectural Digest* France) and the exhibitions that it hosts, *AD Intérieurs* and *AD Collections*.

Her gratitude also goes out to everyone on the *AD* team, whose talent and creativity have made the magazine the most outstanding, most inspiring, and most respected publication in its field.

The New Chic
French Style from Today's Leading Interior Designers
First published in the United States of America
in 2017 by Rizzoli International Publications, Inc.
300 Park Avenue South,
New York, NY 10010
www.rizzoliusa.com

© 2017 Rizzoli International Publications, Inc.

Text
© *Architectural Digest* France

For Architectural Digest

Editorial Direction
Marie Kalt
Cédric Saint André Perrin

Creative Direction
Thibaut Mathieu
Graphic Design
Tiphaine Massard / Cake Design
Iconographic Research
Shirley Doukhan
Juliette Orts

Texts
Marion Bley
Aude de la Conté
Axelle Corty
Oscar Duboÿ
Marina Hemonet
Cédric Saint André Perrin
Françoise Claire-Prodhon
Translation
David Jaggard
Editing
Renaud Legrand

For Rizzoli

Publisher
Charles Miers
Editorial Direction
Catherine Bonifassi
Editor
Daniel Melamud
Copy Editor
Victorine Lamothe
Production
Maria Pia Gramaglia
Editorial Coordination
CASSI EDITION, Vanessa Blondel,
Audrey Gregorczyk

This book has been set in
Camille
Malou Verlomme
Bahamontès
Mathieu Reguer / Fonderie Longtype

Library of Congress Control Number
2016956269

ISBN
978-0-8478-5823-1
2018 2019 2020 / 10 9 8 7 6 5 4 3 2

Printed in China